ACTIVITY IN THE PRIMARY SCHOOL

Music

Activity in the Primary School Series

ACTIVITY IN THE PRIMARY SCHOOL

Music

by

Muriel Hart

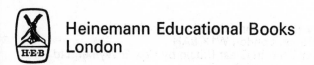

Heinemann Educational Books
London

Heinemann Educational Books Ltd
LONDON MELBOURNE EDINBURGH TORONTO
AUCKLAND SINGAPORE JOHANNESBURG
IBADAN NAIROBI HONG KONG
KUALA LUMPUR NEW DELHI

ISBN 0 435 80606 8

Published by Heinemann Educational Books Ltd
48 Charles Street, London W1X 8AH
Printed Offset Litho in Great Britain by Cox & Wyman Ltd
London, Fakenham and Reading

Contents

SOUNDS TO INVESTIGATE

how sounds are made,
transmitted and heard

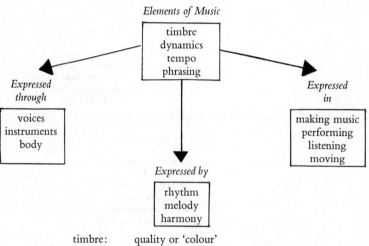

Elements of Music

timbre
dynamics
tempo
phrasing

Expressed through

voices
instruments
body

Expressed in

making music
performing
listening
moving

Expressed by

rhythm
melody
harmony

timbre: quality or 'colour'
dynamics: levels   loud – soft
                                    increasing – decreasing
tempo: speed   fast – slow
                                    increasing – decreasing
phrasing: shape and balance
                                    repetition
                                    question and answer
                                    similarity
                                    contrast
                                    climax

rhythm: duration   (long – short
melody: pitch   (high – low
harmony: combining of pitch

                                    (two or more tunes
                                    (chords

INSTRUMENTS

untuned and
tuned percussion,
improvised instruments,
recorders, melodicas,
violins, cellos,
guitar, mouth-organs

/

CREATIVITY

exploring sound,
using it in songs,
stories, movement,
improvisation,
simple composition –
individual and corporate

INTEGRATION

with English, art,
movement, other cultures,
other periods, etc.

——SINGING

fants – nursery rhymes
   activity songs
   singing games
   songs for fun
   'interest' songs
   hymns – carols
iors – traditional, folk,
tional, contemporary
ngs; rounds, canons,
   descants

SOUNDS TO MAKE

body percussion,
sound of words,
rhythm instruments,
pitched instruments

SOUNDS TO HEAR

natural sounds,
contemporary sounds,
instrumental and
vocal sounds,
music on records,
radio and tape

SOUNDS TO INTERPRET

in movement and dance,
art
creative writing

SOUNDS TO INVESTIGATE

how sounds are made,
transmitted and heard

LITERACY

gh rhythmic and
lodic patterns,
onic sol-fa,
 rhythm names,
gnition games,
 om instruments

Acknowledgements

I wish to acknowledge my indebtedness to numerous individuals, whose names it would be impossible to list, but who, during my years of teaching, have markedly influenced my thinking, my approach and my practice.

In particular I wish to thank Mrs Mary Lowden (Senior Lecturer in Dance, Brighton College of Education), for all her generous help in the chapter on movement, and without whom it could not have been written. In addition I am indebted to the ideas and work of Carl Orff and also to certain suggestions contained in *Music Reading for Young Children* (Windebank); *Musical Instruments in the Classroom* (Winters); *Creative Singing* (Evans) and *The Composer in the Classroom* (R. Murray Schafer). My grateful thanks are also due to the teachers and children with whom I have worked who have not only taught me much but who continue to stimulate new ideas.

Chapter One: Introduction

My experience has taught me that completely unmusical children are very rare and that nearly every child is at some point
accessible and educable ...

Carl Orff (trans. Margaret Murray)

There is no absolute right or wrong regarding the teaching of music
beyond the general statement that when children are interested and
responsive it is right, and when they are bored and uninvolved it is
wrong – except perhaps to add that when the teaching which elicits
interest and response is also informed, then it is as it should be, and the
children concerned are fortunate indeed.

This book is intended to fulfil a two-fold purpose. First, to assemble
and present in one volume the wide span of musical activity which is
possible within the primary school, together with suggestions as to how
the various aspects might be developed; and secondly to provide at the
same time a certain amount of musical background knowledge for
those who feel their own to be so slight that it prevents them from
even attempting to take any music in school.

Many methods are recommended as being the sure way to successful music-making with children and each has something of value to
contribute, but more often than not the success has come about because
the person who implemented the method was someone able to communicate music to children as a living and vital experience. This serves
to emphasize yet again that the deciding factor in children's response
to learning is, in the final issue, the teacher. Particularly is this so in the
realm of music because of the deeply personal nature of the subject.
Life-long attitudes of pleasure or rejection can result from early musical
experiences at school. These are not always a reflection of the teacher's
advanced or limited musicianship but rather of the relationship and
atmosphere which went with the music. It is one of the truisms of
teaching that for good or ill we are continually communicating what

we are with far greater impact than what we know or say. Therefore music will have the best chance to flourish where its teachers are positive in approach, open-minded, quick to commend and encourage, slow to blame, tolerant and good-humoured – whatever the level of musical qualification they possess.

Lack of musical training need not of necessity be a permanent drawback to a teacher wanting to make music with primary school children. In some ways, it could be turned into an asset. Present-day resources are as available to the teacher as to the children, and anyone re-educating himself, or herself, in music could be in a better position to understand the child's point of view than someone who has long since forgotten what the early stages of music learning were like. It can sometimes happen that people with a great love of music and quite advanced musical accomplishment make musical experience for children a rather dull affair. The remedy may mean having to re-think what is being done in music and why, and then being prepared to adapt and change according to current needs and resources. Creativity in the classroom applies not only to those who learn, but also to those who teach.

Although enjoyment and practical activity are implicit in primary-school music, this does not exclude the need for having definite aims and objectives. There must be opportunity for musical knowledge and experience to grow, otherwise, the long-term value is seriously affected. This continuity of progress is not always easy to achieve.

A possible solution is to have one specially qualified person to take all the music throughout a school, as is the case in most secondary schools. However, apart from the fact that the demand for such teachers would far exceed supply, there are certain disadvantages, particularly for children of infant and lower junior age. A music specialist who takes children once or twice a week can only present music in a somewhat piecemeal and detached fashion. The foundations of music reading cannot begin to happen under these conditions. Also, someone who is outside the individual class situation is greatly handicapped in trying to relate music to other aspects of classroom life, and music can then very easily become a mere adjunct to normal activities instead of an integral part of them. The teacher–children relationship may tend to be on a somewhat superficial level, and for infants this is far from ideal. If, on the other hand, a choice has to be made between having no music at all and having it taken by a music specialist, obviously the second alternative is better.

One of the aims of this book, however, is to try to persuade the majority of infant teachers and many junior teachers that present-day approaches to music are well within their capacity and that in using them they will be helping to extend and quicken children's musical education to a marked degree.

This of course is not to underestimate the benefit of having a person available who is able to combine a good teaching approach with special musical ability. Such a person is not only invaluable for directing the more advanced forms of music-making such as choirs and instrumental groups, but also for advising, supervising and co-ordinating all the music within a school. Where, however, there is no such person, it is suggested that to achieve some kind of progress, an overall plan be worked out and agreed between members of staff in voluntary consultation so that children's musical development is not impeded by lack of liaison between one year group and another, or between one department and another.

The various ideas and suggestions which follow have not been classified according to particular age groups because their appropriateness or otherwise is subject to so many variables. If, for instance, children in the middle of a junior school have had no previous experience in using classroom instruments or of learning notation, then the early stages of these two aspects will apply to them as to younger children. The content of the material used may have to be adapted and the rate of progress adjusted, but the principle and basic approach will be the same. As some kind of general guide, however, I have made a summary at the end of this chapter of what might be expected from children who had been taught under ideal conditions by ideal teachers throughout the primary school years. If it seems that some chapters deal only with the beginning stages this is because these first steps are the most vital. Once they have been successfully negotiated, the way ahead lies wide open – what has been learnt is then absorbed into use. In presenting this compendium of suggestions it is not imagined or intended that they should all be used in any one situation, but rather that teachers will find among them something useful which they can adapt and develop according to their own interests and skills and within the limited amount of time and energy at their disposal.

I suppose anyone who is sufficiently interested in music to read this book is unlikely to need any statement to convince him of the value of music in the life of an individual or of a school. Nevertheless, as a salutary reminder, here is an explicit summing-up of the value to both.

To the individual

A true musician in the course of his musical experience will have spent an inestimable number of hours in the following ways:

    in keen mental activity;
    in cultivating aural sensitivity and discrimination;
    in muscular skills and co-ordination, often of a very complex kind;
    in intense concentration;
    in emotional involvement;
    in imaginative understanding;
    in perseverance;
    in appreciating historical development of style;
    in a variety of social contacts;
    in giving and receiving pleasure.

Musical activity then, in its widest concept, involves the whole person – physically, mentally, spiritually and socially.

To the community

'History shows that the arts in their own right are a necessity to civilized man, but possibly their greatest advantage is that they act as a catalyst in the general life of a school. So long as they are treated not as an academic exercise but with vitality, they appear to release energy and add sparkle and inventiveness to the general life of the school. They pay for themselves by quickening the whole tempo . . .' (Stewart Mason, formerly Director of Education for Leicester).

Summary of musical activities for different age groups

Nursery and young infants

Singing: songs with 'catchy' tunes, simple words, easy repetitive choruses; actions (using hands, fingers, body movement in imitation of animals, people's work, etc.); nursery rhymes; simple singing games.

All these can be interspersed throughout the day so that singing becomes as natural and spontaneous as speech. Songs to be learnt from the teacher's voice and sung with her (preferably unaccompanied or with guitar), as mothers once sang to their children.

Instrumental: opportunity for 'sound'-play (cf. need for sand and water play) from a varied collection of sound-producing material assembled in a music corner (content and times of use may need to be discreetly controlled by the teacher because of noise factor for everyone); limited amount of tuned percussion (e.g. pentatonic scale of chime bars and one xylophone).

Listening: the hearing of very short extracts of rhythmic and lively music at odd moments during the day (between other activities or while doing something else of a quiet nature).

Creativity: the exploration of sound; simple use of appropriate-sounding material or instrument in illustrating single feature of a story or poem.

Movement: opportunity for plenty of free and imaginative movement in response to simple percussion sounds and gay rhythmic music.

Top infants and lower juniors

Singing: repertoire to extend to traditional songs, songs from other countries, songs for fun, songs linked with natural interests of this age (e.g. animals, people, things around us, etc.); beginning of interpretation in understanding character and mood of song; some simple vocal improvisation (either freely or linked with pentatonic scale or tonic sol-fa); unaccompanied, or accompanied by guitar, auto-harp, children's own use of tuned and untuned percussion, piano (if well played).

Instrumental: more specific use of tuned and untuned percussion as accompaniment to songs; more extended use of percussion in illustrating stories and in rhythm and pitch development; beginning of recorder playing.

Listening: to own music-making; continued use of music for hearing; beginning of specific listening to music which has direct appeal (rhythmic, tuneful, single instruments, etc.) for a few minutes only; increased awareness of sounds around us.

Creativity: continued exploration of sound; extension of own music-making for stories, plays, poems, etc. and for sound pictures/patterns/sound collage; improvisation using wider range of tuned percussion instruments, based on word patterns and combining sounds from pentatonic scale; simple tune building with or without words.

Movement: development of ideas mutual to music and movement such as phrase, dynamics, tempo, etc.; making of own dance sequences with partner or in small groups; combining individual use of percussion.

Notation: introduction of written rhythmic patterns ♩ ♫ ♩; outline of melodic pattern, introduction of stave, and limited pitched notes.

Middle to top juniors

Singing: increased variety and style of song; international folk songs; national songs; modern songs; rounds and canons; descants; simple two-part; specially composed song sequences with instrumental accompaniment and dramatic content; interpretation and musical 'shaping' of songs; extended vocal improvisation (phrases, question–answer, etc.) and in more than one part; accompaniment – tuned and untuned percussion, guitar, piano.

Instrumental: more advanced use of tuned and untuned percussion with progression from pentatonic scale to use of full scale and chords; classroom ensemble; recorder ensemble (descant, treble, tenor); instruments such as guitar, violin, 'cello, some wind, e.g. clarinet/brass.

Listening: to a wider variety of music and for a longer period of listening (about 10 minutes maximum); to music performed by other children; to concerts by students or small groups of professional musicians.

Creativity: more advanced improvisation in groups as background music, in original setting of words, in making words and music for simple cantatas or operettas, in instrumental and/or vocal ensembles, in original music for dance.

Movement: development of movement response with interpretation of original music and of selected music; combining of groups in class dance sequences; in dramatic interpretation.

Notation: recognition and use of rhythmic notation; recognition and use of one and a half octaves from the stave; both for instrumental and/or vocal performance.

Integration: with English science, art, history, other cultures, etc.

Chapter Two: Classroom Instrumental Music

There is no need for any teacher these days to equate inability to play the piano with inability to take music, or lack of hall time and space with lack of suitable facilities. It is true that there was a time when these two factors certainly determined whether or not children participated in any form of music-making, but that time has now passed.

Various music broadcasts on radio and television go a long way towards meeting the needs of many schools in this direction and often include in their programmes suggestions for the use of tuned percussion instruments such as xylophones, glockenspiels and chime bars, together with untuned percussion, both orthodox and improvised. Such instruments need not be restricted to use with these specific broadcasts alone. They offer scope for a wide range of musical activity within a classroom situation, particularly for the teacher who may feel diffident about presenting music in its more traditional forms, yet would like to provide children with interesting and lively musical experiences.

This chapter gives detailed information about such instruments and also some of the ways in which they can be used.

CLASSROOM INSTRUMENTS

Tuned percussion

The increasing availability in recent years of tuned percussion instruments has meant that it has now become possible for every child from the infant school onwards to have access to a pitched musical instrument of good quality sound with a playing technique within everyone's capacity, thus enabling melodic and harmonic concepts to develop alongside that of rhythm. In some areas the cost of providing these instruments in sufficient numbers may be thought too high. There may be a need to persuade and convince those in authority that by making such provision they are enabling many more children to achieve a sound and satisfying musical education and this is something which could affect future generations. Money, like time, is usually spent according to people's interests and priorities, and it is more than likely that with sufficient motivation, enough money would be found. **Chime bars** are probably the most generally useful instrument and certainly the most suitable as a first choice. Their advantages are that they are portable and take up little storage space; they can be used by a number of children at the same time; they produce a very agreeable sound and are very easy to play; they can be played while moving or while watching something or somebody; and they are the least expensive, giving good service for a number of years. In an infant school there should be at least one set of chime bars per class (or class equivalent), that is, one octave of the scale of C plus top D and E, an extra G and an F sharp.

The cost when distributed between members of a class and divided by the years of use, is minimal. In a junior school, the compass of notes should be extended at either end, all chromatic notes added, and more sets made available.

Xylophones. It is of paramount importance to have instruments of good musical quality. The wooden bars (which should be detachable) give a pleasing contrast in timbre to chime bars and glockenspiels and the range includes soprano, alto and bass. The quality of sound produced by a good alto xylophone is somewhat akin to that of the treble recorder and the width of the bars is such that young children can play on them without being hampered by difficulty in aiming the beater. The bass xylophone, although the most expensive, has a very fine and distinctive sound and gives an added dimension to ensemble work.

Glockenspiels. As the name indicates, they have a bell-like sound, rather similar to that of chime bars, but with longer-lasting resonance. It is best to have instruments with a damper device, otherwise the sound can become too blurred. The soprano glockenspiel, though small in volume, adds an effective top register of sound but it is not so easy for infants to play because of the narrowness of the bars. As with xylophones, the separate bars should lift off and the right kind of beaters be provided. A further range of this tone colour is introduced by the use of the metallaphone.

In playing all these tuned percussion instruments, children should understand from the beginning that the 'ball' of the beater must bounce, otherwise the bar cannot vibrate freely to resonate as it should.

Xylophones and glockenspiels are more expensive items than chime bars, but they probably have a longer span of usefulness, particularly those with the full chromatic range of notes, and are therefore an investment. It may take a period of several years properly to equip a school depending on the amount of money and storage space available.

Untuned Percussion

A plea is sometimes made that children should always and only be provided with good quality percussion instruments and certainly as far as cymbals are concerned this is indisputable. But the age of the children and the purpose for which the instruments are being used should also be taken into account. The usual purpose, for instance, of good quality orchestral percussion instruments, such as snare drums, tambourines, full-sized triangles, castanets, cymbals, etc., is to provide an extra dimension of timbre to orchestral music where one of each is sufficient to balance some seventy to eighty other fully developed musical instruments, all of which are played by experienced adults. Therefore, although there is a place for a few such instruments in each class, especially towards the top of a junior school for combined tuned and untuned ensemble playing, I would suggest it is a limited place. There are several other instruments available – in addition to the main orchestral percussion instruments already referred to – which are more within the playing capacity and tonal requirement of primary children. These are listed below together with an approximate indication of the proportion of instruments that will give balance and contrast.

Suggestions for untuned percussion instruments

tambour	I
snare drum (medium size)	I
tuneable drum	2 or 3
Chinese drums (4 in a set)	I or 2 sets

bongoes	2 or 3
tambourines	2 or 3
triangles – not too large	3 or 4
maracas	2 or 3
cymbals – size according to size of children	1 pair
suspended cymbal	1
castanets	2 pairs
resi-resi/guiro (a kind of scraper)	1
wood blocks	2
two-toned wood blocks	2 or 3
Indian cymbals	several
stick jingles	several
sleigh bells	several
claves	several pairs
wire brushes and a variety of beaters	

Improvised or 'home-made' percussion
Before giving details of this kind of percussion, it might be as well to reconsider the probable origin of musical instruments. It seems very likely that primitive man discovered, sometimes by accident and sometimes by experiment and ingenuity, that sounds could be produced from a variety of objects around him. First, from his own body, by clapping and stamping, etc., and then from things very near to hand such as wood, bone, gourds, stones, stems of plants, tautened skins, etc. In the same way, children, who it is acknowledged often re-enact certain historical processes, are using what is imminent to their hands and experience when they make use of adapted articles of domestic hardware etc. as improvised instruments. Some of the advantages offered by such instruments are: a wide variety of timbre or palette of sound colours; virtually no cost; they are expendable and replaceable; no technique is required; they are adaptable to all sizes of hands (important for infants); can alert the mind and ear to the potential of any and every sound; train aural selectivity; and they include the span of basic percussion elements (e.g. instruments for tapping, shaking, jingling, ringing).

Some children enjoy making a home-made instrument look attractive by painting or decorating it, but if this entails undue delay in using it, do without. A baby is just as happy with a spoon to bang as with an ornate toy – it is making the sound that matters most. Older children may like to experiment with making their own more sophisticated versions.

Suggestions for improvised instruments
for tapping:

jam tins with plastic lids
flat plastic bottles
yoghurt cartons tapped on the base with sticks
2 yoghurt cartons tapped together
coconut shells
walnuts
pebbles/flints
pairs of sticks of varying thickness
plastic chair-castor cups, etc.

for shaking:

containers: yoghurt cartons with lids,
small tins, two shells, type-writer ribbon boxes, talcum and hand-cream plastic bottles (especially with long necks)
fillings: rice, sago, small stones, dried peas, bean pods, buttons, screws, marbles, nails, seeds, paper clips, broken-up macaroni, etc.

for jingling:

bottle tops on wire fixed to a wood stick (similar to sleigh bells)
milk tops strung together or made into bunches

for scraping:

serrated wood or bamboo (bamboo often obtainable from carpet shops)
ridged plastic squash bottles
corrugated plastic
sandpaper blocks (beware of friction)

for ringing:

cow bells and the like
metal tubing
glasses
bottles filled with varying amounts of water

semi-pitched:
   pudding basins
   some saucepans, lids and frying pans
   flower pots suspended on a frame by string attached to a button or
   a small stick

Where to keep the instruments

The practical problem of lack of adequate space is one confronting
many teachers and must be mentioned since it is often the reason why
these instruments are not more widely used – especially the tuned
percussion instruments.

Some schools may be able to set aside a special room in which all
the instruments can be kept and made permanently available to the
children. Advantages of such an arrangement are that the sound
resulting from children experimenting and practising is not so likely to
interfere with other people and other activities, and that the instruments can be used constantly. Disadvantages are that the number of
children in a school who can use the instruments at any one time is
somewhat limited and that music cannot be spontaneously integrated
into the general curriculum of the day if the instruments are elsewhere.

Occasionally instruments are kept in distant cupboards and corri-
dors. This is not a solution but a deterrent that will, in time, affect the
most well-intentioned and enthusiastic teacher. The value of instruments is not in possessing them but in using them.

Untuned percussion
This is the simpler to accommodate and can be kept on a table, a shelf,
a window ledge, in various sized boxes (preferably shallow), or suspended from holders affixed to wall pin-boarding which is within the
children's reach. Smaller items, such as claves and shakers, could perhaps be kept in desks or children's own trays. Alternatively they can
all be kept together in a specially designed trolley and if there is more
than one floor or level in a school, it is to be hoped that eventually
sufficient trolleys will be procured and equipped to meet this situation.

Tuned percussion
Chime bars can be set out on trays so that they can be easily distributed
or, when necessary, moved as a unit. They should not be kept in

separate cardboard boxes except in a music shop. Beaters are best kept in a narrow, upright container. Xylophones and glockenspiels are less easy to house in a classroom. The solution will vary according to individual situations and resourcefulness. Because of their greater cost, there is often concern about the possibility of damage. Again, the likelihood of this is something that will vary from school to school, but the benefit gained from having the instruments available to everyone would seem to outweigh the risk of damage by a few. In any case, children should be helped to understand that all musical instruments warrant careful treatment since much skill, time and money has been expended in producing them. Older juniors might find it of interest to investigate how instruments are made and the ways in which they have developed over the centuries.

Lastly, by providing these instruments and encouraging children to use them as much as possible, allowance must be made for the amount of sound which will result. Be realistic about it for yourself, the children and the rest of the school. Select certain times and places for practising to take place. If necessary, arrange a rota system so that all the children who want to may have a turn. Try to come to an amicable agreement with other members of staff. For without doubt it seems a basic need of children to go through the primitive stage of making sounds just for the sake of it, and it is only when they have been given adequate opportunity to do this that they can then begin to use instruments in a more controlled and purposeful way within a musical context.

USES OF CLASSROOM INSTRUMENTS

Untuned percussion
1 accompaniment to songs
2 awareness of timbre
3 pictures and patterns in sound, illustrating stories, poems, events, ideas

Tuned percussion
1 free improvisation
2 tunes illustrating stories, etc.
3 tunes to word patterns, leading on to songs or instrumental music

4 rhythmic development, use of words, ensemble playing
5 movement
6 notation of rhythm

4 tunes that go together – ensemble
5 development of pitch
6 song accompaniment – chords
7 notation of pitch

Although the two forms of percussion have been separated in order to show the possibilities within each, it is not intended that in actual practice they should always be kept separate, but rather that they should be combined whenever it seems suitable.

UNTUNED PERCUSSION

Accompaniment to songs

Untuned percussion
To include some of these instruments as an accompaniment to children's singing adds interest and variety. The choice of instrument will be influenced by what is suitable for a particular song having considered the words, the mood and the musical style. Children can be helped to select the appropriate instruments with these factors in mind.

Always be aware of the need for balance so that the singing is not spoilt or overpowered by an accompaniment that is too elaborate or too difficult. Also remember that however simple the instrument may be, it is being used for a musical purpose and not as an outlet for a child's aggression or inhibitions.

Suggested progression of rhythmic patterns
This is not necessarily related to the age of the children but to their ability, stage of development and previous experience. Keep in mind that sufficient practice in the simpler patterns is essential before attempting the more difficult ones. All the patterns can be learnt in the first place by everyone, through the use of body percussion (i.e. clapping, tapping, slapping, stamping, etc.) but eventually only a few children at any one time should play them on instruments.

(*a*) the beat or pulse – basic, especially for young children, but limited in musical interest

(the single rhythmic sound corresponds to the 'drone' in pitch development)

(*b*) alternate beat

(*c*) first beat of the bar

(*d*) pattern of the tune (tends to be rather heavy as an accompaniment pattern) e.g., 'Hot cross buns'

(*e*) pattern based on part of the song – probably using words from it, e.g., 'Baa baa black sheep'

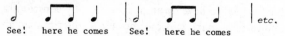

Have you a – ny wool   Have you a – ny wool   etc.

(this repeated pattern is a rhythmic ostinato corresponding to a melodic ostinato in pitch development)

(*f*) a repeated independent pattern which can be learnt by the association of words or by reading it from notation (see Chapter 8), e.g., 'Bobby Shaftoe'

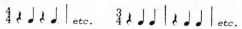

See!   here he comes   See!   here he comes   etc.

(*g*) 'off' beats

(h) syncopated rhythm

♪ ♪♪ ♩ | ♪ ♪♪ ♩ | *etc.*

(i) a mixture of the above, including rests

♩ ♪♪ ♩ | ♫♩ ♫♩ | – | ♬♫♩ |

(this more extensive range of rhythmic pattern corresponds to melody in pitch development)

The choice of pattern must of course bear some relation to the musical content of the individual song. It can also be used as an introduction or as a link between verses and some of the patterns can be combined. Different groups of instruments can be used to accompany the various verses but it is not advisable to have more than three differing types playing at once, except perhaps for an occasional cymbal or cow-bell to highlight a feature of the music.

Awareness of timbre

Timbre in music is the equivalent of colour and texture in art. But whereas in art both children and adults make use of the same raw materials for the expression of their individual ideas, in music they do not.

The adult composer has at his disposal the varying tonal qualities of a wide selection of highly developed instruments with which to give his music contrast and character, blend and balance. Children, on the other hand, if they are to find a way of expressing themselves in terms of music, must make use of other resources of sound. Hence the importance of classroom instruments, both tuned and untuned, with the greater variety of timbre being provided by the untuned and improvised instruments. From their very first experience of a music corner, children can be helped to develop aural awareness by consciously listening to the sounds they make and by learning to discriminate and choose for a particular purpose. Claves and woodblocks, shakers and stones tapped together are not just noises. They each have an individuality of timbre which can be recognized, distinguished and exploited for a genuine musical purpose. They can be grouped for contrast and similarity, for dynamics and climax, for mood and character, and their range continually increased.

This awareness of timbre is much encouraged by the imaginative use of instruments in illustrating parts of stories, poems, dramatic situations, events, ideas and in accompanying and stimulating dance movement.

3 Pictures and patterns in sound

The making of these will depend almost entirely on the interest and attitude of the class teacher, because only he or she knows the possibilities for this which can emerge from the many other aspects of learning and living contained in a child's day. If, for instance, something can be illustrated in art or craft, it is probably worth considering whether it could also be illustrated in music. This does not imply that the sound element should be artificially forced into any and every situation, but there are occasions when certain stories, poems, events, etc., lend themselves to this form of expression. There are two main aspects: (i) pictorial (or representational sound) – corresponding to programme music in which a subjective idea is conveyed in addition to the sound itself; (ii) abstract (or patterns in sound) – corresponding to pure music in which the sound is heard for its own sake only.

(i) Pictures in sound

One of the aims of this approach is to stimulate children's imagination. The sounds therefore which are freely selected for this purpose will often be non-rhythmic since they will accord with an incident in a story or poem, or be an impression of a character, a mood or an idea. At the most elementary level this may mean choosing an instrument with the nearest matching sound to the real thing. For example: for footsteps – tapping with fingers or knuckles on a tambour; for a door slamming – loud bang on a drum; for horses hooves – coconut shells; for a cuckoo call – the notes G to E. Very soon, however, the instruments can be used to express something more – for instance, the several ways of moving, such as dancing, leaping, creeping, limping, galloping, chasing, sliding, spinning, wandering. Gradually children discover how to consider the essence of what they are describing and to convey it through the use of instrumental sound. In making a picture in sound of an animal, such as an elephant, a squirrel, a snake or a tortoise, think about the size of it, its type of movement, its appearance, its characteristics, whether it always behaves in the same way, where and how it lives, etc., because these will affect the choice of instruments and the manner in which they are played (e.g. an enraged elephant in the jungle, a mischievous monkey in the treetops, a frightened mouse in a garage).

Suggestions of subjects for 'sound' pictures
  animals: wild, farm and domestic, mothers and their young
  birds: eagle, ostrich, penguin, humming bird; flight
  insects: grasshopper, beetle, caterpillar, moth
  people: an old man, a clumsy giant, a frightened child, a haughty
      queen, a vicious troll, a spaceman, a gang of pirates/smugglers
  things: forms of transport, machines
  natural occurrences: elements of fire, earth, water; the seasons; the
      wind, the sea; volcano, tornado, avalanche, glacier; desert,
      prairie, jungle, icefield; under the earth, under the sea, in space
  expeditions: to a farm, fairground, circus, station, quay, factory
  moods: excitement, anger, fear, contentment, weariness, aggression,
      laziness
  fantasy: witches, wizards, ogres, spells, dragons; inventors; other
      worlds; fantasy creatures
  activities: the school day; life on board a sailing ship; camping

Story illustration
These single subject ideas can, of course, be incorporated into a story format using either something that is well known or something that is the original work of a child.

The following example is one way in which a whole class could eventually be involved in using classroom instruments to illustrate parts of a story. It is the familiar tale of the competition between the sun and the wind in which each tries to prove his superiority by making a man take off his coat. Time should be given to considering and choosing the most appropriate sounds and to some preparatory work in groups. Voices are also used.

The sound of the wind
   a soft breeze increasing to a gale
   instruments: voices ('whoo-oo-whee-ee', etc.) increasing in pitch and
      intensity, subsiding and increasing again (i.e. dynamics of soft–
      loud, crescendo–dimuendo); blowing across open top of plastic
      bottle.

The effect of the wind:
   in the town: doors slamming, windows rattling, telegraph wires
      'whistling', footsteps hurrying, roof slates falling
   in parks: leaves rustling, twigs snapping, branches breaking
   at sea: surging and crashing of waves, suction sound of the shingle,
      pebbles being tossed about
   in a storm: raindrops increasing to deluge, thunder
   instruments: voices ('sh-sh-sh') crescendo and decrescendo, tambour,
      claves, shakers with soft sound (rice/sand), with loud sound
      (pebbles/stones), stick jingles, tambourines for tapping or shaking,
      bottle-top jingles, fingers on paper/foil/drum, etc., sheet of card-
      board

The sun:
   nature of sunshine: continuous warmth and light which spread
      everywhere i.e. small beginnings gradually increasing in strength
      and intensity to a final climax
   instruments: ringing, vibrating sounds which spread – triangle,
      Indian cymbals, suspended cymbal with soft stick, chime bars
      (varied notes of pentatonic scale or of chord), glockenspiel (es-
      pecially the soprano using glissando), etc.

Such sound effects can be interpolated at the appropriate moment
during the final telling of the story. Alternatively, instruments can
sometimes be used to provide a background to the acting or miming
of a story. It is not often practical, however, for individual voices to
try to speak against the sound of several instruments – other ways
should be found of combining them. Since all class teachers have their
own story resources I have not thought it necessary to make a list of
suggestions, but would just mention in passing that the world's folk-
tales, myths and legends provide very suitable material for this kind

of illustrative approach, stories such as the Pied Piper, Pandora, Persephone. Similarly, because poetry is so much a matter of individual preference and the choice so wide, I have refrained from singling out a particular poem for treatment in this way. The basic principle however is the same and the sounds can be used either as background to the choral speaking of the words or as partial accompaniment to certain lines, as an instrumental comment on the words before or after they are spoken, or as a link between stanzas – not always of the same duration.

(ii) Patterns in sound

This could be considered a somewhat freer approach and the suggestions here will be more in the nature of guidelines since whatever is done must depend on a willingness and wish by children and teacher alike to explore and experiment with a variety of sound resources. The comparative ease of producing sounds on both pitched and unpitched percussion instruments makes them particularly suitable for this kind of creativity but there is no reason why other instruments should not also be included. In many primary schools there are children who can play recorder, piano, guitar, violin, 'cello, melodica, trumpet, mouth-organ, etc. and all these can be involved, if need be, in this creative approach. Most instruments can also be played in more than one way and it is worth experimenting with this, as it can produce a different and sometimes unexpected effect. There is a strong link in this approach with pattern-making and collage work in art, and with the making of body shapes and movement sequences in dance, and sometimes one form of expression can be a stimulus to the other.

Suggestions for making sound patterns

(a) Transfer the rhythmic pattern of various words and phrases to groups of instruments combining them in several ways to give instrumental texture (see pp. 30 and 33).

(b) Assemble a mixed assortment of instrumental (and/or vocal) sound as in assembling materials for collage. Use them singly, in twos and threes, in groups – in sequence (a series of sounds following one after the other) – antiphonally (as in conversation). For example, a slow, then frenzied pattern on a drum – silence – isolated and irregular notes on a melodic instrument interspersed with repeated, insistent

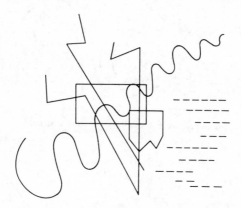

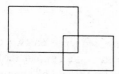

Tightly packed sounds –
rhythmic or melodic

Sharp uneven pattern
or angular tune

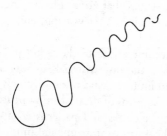

Sequential pattern beginning loud and
decreasing / beginning low and getting
higher or vice versa

Separate sharp sounds

a cumulative pattern involving various strands

rhythmic fragment on a triangle – a 'chasing' sequence on two contrasting instruments – a combined unison pattern – a cymbal clash.

(c) Develop a sequence from a single idea by the use of repetition, imitation, contrast, cumulative effect, silence, increase and/or decrease in speed and volume, climax.

(d) Use sounds to give the effect of shapes that are solid, twisting, spiralling, spiky, curved, isolated, overlapping, interweaving, etc.

When children and teachers once become aware of the many possibilities offered by this approach and of the raw materials of sound that are available all around, there is no limit to what resourcefulness, ingenuity and imagination can produce in terms of musical enjoyment. The palette from which to paint these pictures and patterns is unrestricted and individual. Moreover, this form of instrumental music-making employs the same elements as those used in more advanced musical composition, such as choice of timbre, dynamics, tempo, mood, climax and so on.

If, however, children are to be able to use instruments in this way, they must of course have access to them and also be given opportunity and encouragement to experiment and work out their ideas in their own time and way. This does not exclude wise and careful guidance on the part of the teacher who must see to it that *children always listen to what they do*, and as they become older and more experienced, learn to assess and compare it, revise and listen again.

It is an aspect of music-making which is primarily for the individual and the small group even if sometimes it ends up as a corporate project. Some schools may find this relatively easy to achieve if there is group and team-teaching and a free timetable, but others may find it quite difficult to organize. In both cases, consideration does have to be given to the aural susceptibilities of the rest of the school.

The implementation of these ideas is a longterm process and much of its success depends on providing the right stimulus. A sense of achievement too is important, and it is good to have an end product which all can listen to.

4 Rhythmic development

This section deals first with the basic principles of rhythm before going on to describe the use of instruments in developing this aspect of music.

Most children have an innate sense of rhythmic pulse, but always be prepared for the few who seem to find difficulty in expressing it. Playing rhythmic patterns on a variety of instruments with other children not only helps to affirm this sense but also affords pleasure and enjoyment.

Always give plenty of rhythmic practice first through the use of body percussion.* Not only is this easier than even the simplest instrument but it ensures that every child feels rhythm as a physical experience. Without this, verbal explanation and written symbols have much less significance. This is one of the reasons why those who try to learn the musical language at post primary-school stage, often find it so difficult. They are having to accept the meaning of the written symbol through a mental process only, without first knowing the physical experience. They often feel, understandably, that physical participation as expressed through body movement or body percussion is something which belongs to an earlier stage – but nothing can replace this. If it

* See list of definitions p. 45.

could be guaranteed that by the age of nine, every child had received this valuable early experience whereby the basic concepts of rhythm are gradually absorbed, one direct benefit would be that the progress of every pupil learning to play a traditional instrument would be at least twice as fast, and the task of every teacher halved!

Rhythmic concept
Underpinning all rhythmic pattern is the repeated beat or pulse. Although the pulse of our heart-beat can be felt (and incidentally, children often find it hard to find), it cannot be heard, but the sound of footsteps walking and running can be, and because of its familiarity, this is often used as the starting point for the understanding of rhythmic values. This regularity of rhythm is also very noticeable in the movement of wild animals when traversing long distances.

In analysis, the three main durations of sound from which all subsequent rhythmic patterns develop are as follows:

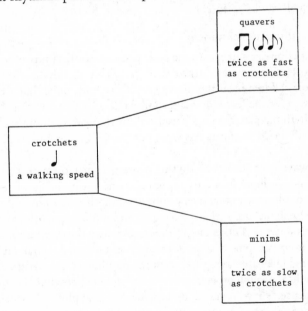

Knowing these is the musical equivalent of knowing the components of ten on which all further forms of calculating are based.

Crotchets

Walking footsteps provide an accurately related sound and young children respond to the stimulus of subjective ideas.

Listen to the sound of Peter's feet as he walks round the room (make sure he is wearing shoes that are audible).

Make the same sound with your hands (the more ways the children can experience it, the better).

Clap it, tap it;

pretend your hands are wearing plimsolls, outdoor shoes, heavy boots;

make the footsteps come from a distance, pass the window and go away (one way of achieving this is to begin by using one finger and then add a finger at a time, culminating with clapping cupped hands);

make your fingers walk on the palm of the other hand, on the table, along your arm, down your leg;

tap your toes on the floor;

move your feet inside your shoes as if they were walking (this corresponds to crotchet rests);

slap your sides;

if you can, click your fingers;

slide the palms of your hands against each other;

and say 'good – strong – foot – steps

walk – ing brisk – ly'.

A crotchet tune: 'The Ash Grove' (in spite of three beats to a bar) or 'Quand trois poules'.

Quavers:

Running or trotting are useful parallels but from the beginning the essential feature to establish is the relationship between the two patterns, i.e. that quavers are twice as fast as crotchets. They must be heard and felt to fit with each other.

Say and clap:

Children running round the playground

(*a*) alternate 4 stamped crotchets (good strong footsteps) and 8 clapped quavers (children running round the playroom)

(*b*) combine the stamps with the claps

(*c*) tap 4 crotchets with one hand on knee or table then 8 quavers with the other hand

(*d*) combine the hands for alternate bars of crotchets

(*e*) combine throughout

Always keep a regular pulse sounding somewhere: the tap of the teacher's foot or the click of the fingers, a steady beat tapped on a single percussion instrument or a repeated note on a tuned percussion instrument.

After a little practice it will become evident which children have a natural sense of rhythmic pulse and they can be chosen first to tap out the communal beat. Choose other children as they become confident of doing it correctly.

A quaver tune: 'Bobby Shaftoe'.

Minims:

A relevant analogy in the context of footsteps is less easy here. Perhaps a giant's strides or someone walking uphill while carrying a lot of shopping, or the slow steps of an old man might be appropriate. Whatever the subjective approach chosen, the sound pattern must again relate so that minims are played twice as slowly as crotchets. In clapping minims, instil the habit of swinging the hands to indicate the second silent beat so that from the first there is this awareness of the equivalent two crotchet beats. The sound of clocks is another well-known starting point for illustrating the relativity of note values, e.g.

crotchets	
wall clock	tick tock tick tock
	(normal voice and clap)
minims	
grandfather clock	tock – tock – (deep voice and swing arm to imitate the slow movement of the pendulum)
quavers	
wrist watch	tick-tick-tick-tick-tick-tick-tick-tick (whispered or high-pitched voice and tap with one finger on palm of other hand)

An alternative suggestion when introducing this stage with older children is the sound made by different-sized balls being bounced, e.g.

tennis ball	– crotchets
ping-pong ball	– quavers
football/netball	– minims

Here is a song which provides an apt example of these three note values and their relationship to each other. It is an adaptation of the nursery rhyme 'The Muffin Man'.

When it is known it can be performed in three groups, e.g.

1 singing the words
2 playing the appropriate rhythm
3 moving – walking/running/stepping slowly

1 Tommy was a big strong man, a big strong man,
   a big strong man,
   Tommy was a big strong man who liked to walk
   to work
   Tommy walked along like this . . . on his way to work
   (crotchet accompaniment)
2 Mary was a little girl (repeat)
   Mary was a little girl who went to (. . .) school
   Mary ran along like this . . . on her way to school
   (quaver accompaniment)
3 Trampie was a poor old man (repeat)
   Trampie was a poor old man whose steps were very slow
   Trampie went along like this . . . because he was so old
   (minim accompaniment)

These first conceptions need not take up too much time (although they take up a good deal of space), but laying good and accurate foundations is very important indeed. So make sure at this stage that there is clear understanding of the individual sounds and the relation-ship between them. As children seem to respond more readily when concepts are conveyed through some kind of imagery, use this approach but as soon as their interest has been caught, this pictorial aspect can gradually be discarded. Once these three foundation note values have been firmly grasped, there is little difficulty in proceeding to more advanced patterns.

Use of instruments

Having made rhythmic patterns by using various forms of body per-cussion, each child needs also to make the sound instrumentally. This is where the quieter sound of many of the improvised instruments is an advantage. Begin by giving instruments to only one or two children per group, or getting them to take it in turn, but gradually extend this so that eventually every child has something to play. (This is psychologically important – especially when children begin.) It is possible to include tuned percussion in this by distributing single chime bars taken from the pentatonic scale★ or from the notes of a chord.

Instrumental practice in crotchets:

Decide on a clear method of indicating the moment when each group begins and stops. With young children, the sign for stopping traffic is very effective for ending the sound and this can later be modified to become the final gesture of a conductor's beat.

Set a pulse going, then let each group play one after the other a sequence of crotchets as directed, e.g.

group	1	claves
	2	yoghurt cups tapped with sticks
	3	shakers
(optional)	4	chime bars (C–E–G–A–C)

Alternate by combining groups 1 and 2

2 and 3

1 and 3

and encourage listening to the varying textures of sound.

★ See definition on p. 46.

Practice in crotchets–quavers–minims:

When combining groups, it is easier in the early stages for one group to begin and the other groups to join in, one at a time. Later all the groups can begin at once provided there has been a preparatory indication of the crotchet speed.

Use three groups of instruments with contrasting timbre, e.g.

crotchets	stick jingles
quavers	claves
minims	triangles/Indian cymbals/chime bars
	(to provide continuous sound that
	corresponds to the minim's duration)

jingles begin – claves join in – now the triangles (all end together or one after the other as directed)

Vary the order of entry so that children have practice in relating their own pattern to that of the others. To begin with, they may not all be able to do this, but with a little practice given at frequent intervals they will soon gain the necessary skill. As each child will have been involved in a practical way, individual and permanent understanding of these rhythms will result.

Further development of this aspect is referred to later in this chapter in the section on rhythmic ensemble.

Words and use of instruments:

The rhythmic element in words also provides the basis for subsequent use of various instruments, both tuned and untuned.

Collect a group of words such as the names of children, their pets, their favourite sweets/food/drink, names of towns/cars/plants/football teams/planets, etc., and try to include in the selection words with varying rhythmic patterns. This gives a more interesting effect when transferred to instruments.

Everyone first speaks the words clearly and rhythmically, with conviction, colour and character. This is particularly important when the single words develop into phrases, sayings and poems. Remember that the speaking voice is also an instrument though often misused and neglected as such.

Single words are usually collected in groups of four to make a metric phrase, and often repeated to help establish the sound of the

rhythm and to make a better balance. Later, words can be grouped to
provide five- or seven-beat rhythms. Interest can be added by introducing varying length gaps or rests, e.g.

blackbird kingfisher (click,click) kingfisher yellowhammer

(click,click)   yellowhammer,yellowhammer   owl

When children first begin this 'saying and playing' there are usually
a few who may be saying the pattern of the words while still clapping
the pulse. Such children should be noticed and given individual help
to get it right.

Rhythmic ensemble
Collections of single words can form the basis for rhythmic ensemble
in the following ways.

Rhythmic rounds:
Word patterns which have been spoken, clapped and learnt by everyone can then be spoken and clapped as rounds, in two, three or four
groups. First set the speed.

(*a*) Each group repeats *ad lib.* one word only and joins in when
directed, finishing either together at a given signal, or one group after
the other.

blackbird, blackbird etc.
        kingfisher, kingfisher etc.
                yellowhammer, yellowhammer etc.
                        owl, etc.

(*b*) Allocate one different percussion instrument (tuned and/or untuned) per group as the representative instrumental sound while
remainder of group still claps.

(*c*) Gradually increase the number of instruments to several per
group and finally to one instrument per child.

To avoid overwhelming volume, again make use of the quieter sound
instruments for this work. It is very frustrating for a child to be given

a loud instrument and then continually be told to play it softly. At the same time, do not be afraid to discourage unnecessarily loud playing.

Question and answer:

   (*a*) spoken and clapped
   (*b*) spoken and played
   (*c*) played

Initially, the question can be spoken-and-clapped or spoken-and-played by the teacher and the answer can be spoken-and-clapped-or-played by individual children or by groups. Individual answers can then be repeated by everyone, first vocally, then instrumentally.

   (*i*) What's the time?

          ten o'clock
          half past seven
          twenty past nine
          quarter to eleven

   (*ii*) Where does this train stop please?

          Hassocks
          Haywards Heath
          Victoria

   (*iii*) Tell me the name of some stations in London.

          Victoria
          King's Cross
          London Bridge
          Liverpool Street

   (*iv*) What are you wearing today?

          blue jumper
          orange skirt
          yellow pullover
          jeans

(*v*) Look out of the window and tell me what you see.

houses and sky
chimney pots
television aerials
grass

(*vi*) Let's go to the shops. What shall we buy?

The various answers can be used cumulatively to make longer phrases which, in turn, can lead on to improvised and composed rhythms and tunes.

The separate lines of well-known songs:
Each line's rhythm is repeated and allocated to various instrumental groups

  (*i*) Baa-baa black sheep   tambourines

  (*ii*) one for the little boy   wood blocks

  (*iii*) have you any wool?   drums or equivalent

  (*iv*) lives down our lane   sleigh-bells

The groups need not be equal in number but can vary in size according to the loudness of the instruments used.

Short sayings or rhymes:

Rain, rain go away, come again another day
Fee, fo, fi, fum, I smell the blood of an Englishman
News headlines and weather forecasts, proverbs; advertising jingles; original sentences; current interests.

Dribble the ball down the field

Head the ball now

Kick it – kick it –

G – o – a – l!

All these provide material for instrumental development and group participation.

Varying ways of using instruments

(i)   Each group on its own plays its own pattern twice through, one group after the other.

(ii) Two sets of words joined together extend the phrase. Each group can then play this longer phrase:
      (a) antiphonally (i.e. group 1 – group 2 – group 1 – group 2)
      (b) as a canon (i.e. in two groups with group 2 beginning one or two bars later)
      (c) as a round (as for a canon, but in 3 or 4 groups).

(iii) The whole sequence of patterns can be played through beginning softly and increasing to a final loud note.

(iv) The whole sequence can be played fast – slow; getting gradually quicker – gradually slower

At a later stage, the words can be omitted so that only instrumental sound is heard. Rhythmic development then combines with instrumental composition. Only attempt this, however, when it is certain that everyone can keep together.

Instrumental ensemble playing for children through the use of tuned and untuned percussion instruments is acknowledged to be one of the direct developments inspired by the ideas of Carl Orff. In his approach there are three basic elements for such group music-making which allow for unlimited individual experiment and improvisation. They are:

the drone
a fundamental simple sound which is repeated throughout
the ostinato
a repeated fragment of pattern, of which there can be several
the independent part
individual realization of an extended free pattern

These three elements are unified by the same pulse. They can all be implemented through the use of:

(a) body percussion   ⎫   rhythm
(b) untuned percussion   ⎬   only

(c) tuned percussion   ⎫   rhythm, melody
(d) a combination of the above ⎬   and harmony
                                ⎭

The following examples are given as an indication of this kind of ensemble.

(a) *Body percussion only:*

drone (group 1)
  slap thighs

add ostinato 1 (group 2)

  clap
  stamp

add ostinato 2 (group 3)

  clap
  click fingers

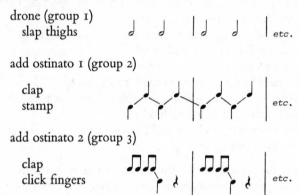

add independent part (teacher and/or individual children) using all forms of body percussion to create an improvised, rhythmic pattern that will combine with the other three parts.

(b) *Untuned percussion only:*

drone (group 1)
  bongoes

add ostinato 1 (group 2)
  claves

add ostinato 3 (group 3)
  shakers

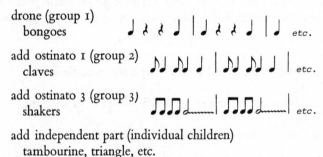

add independent part (individual children)
  tambourine, triangle, etc.

(c) *Tuned percussion only* (details of this are on pp. 7 and 8).
Each and all of these elements is capable of almost unlimited variation. The Orff Schulwerk Books (Schott) contain comprehensive sugges-

tions for this, and the accompanying records – 'Music for Children' – are particularly helpful.

5 Movement

There is considerable opportunity for the use of classroom instruments in providing accompaniment for movement and also in stimulating movement and this is referred to in the chapter on Music and Movement.

6 Notation of rhythm

Instruments fulfil a vital function in the understanding of rhythmic notation since it only becomes individually meaningful for children when they are able to link together the sounds they have been playing with the corresponding visual representation, and when they can transmit into actual sound the rhythms they read and write. For fuller details see Chapter 8 on the written language of music.

TUNED PERCUSSION

1 Free improvisation

This is the first need of any child, irrespective of age, when confronted with a ready-made musical instrument. Most children, for instance, if given the chance to play a piano, will do so immediately, and with obvious pleasure, even though the random notes they play may not be so pleasing to the ear of a listening adult. It seems to satisfy a very strong and basic desire in them to make music, and the provision of tuned percussion instruments in the classroom greatly increases the possibility of this for many more children.

Opportunity will obviously be affected by the number of instruments available and also by the attitude of teachers because of the sound involved. Yet most infant teachers have long since become accustomed to the sounds made by children using carpentry tools, and the sound of free improvisation is certainly quite as tolerable. A partial solution to this problem is only to set out the notes of a pentatonic scale, i.e. for chime bars – the notes C–D–E–G–A, for xylophones and glockenspiels – remove the notes F and B. This will mean that whichever notes are being played there is at least no unpleasant discord. Fortunately, because of the relatively easy technique of these instruments, children progress quite quickly to the stage of wanting more ordered sounds and of being able to organize them into recognizable musical forms.

2 Tunes illustrating stories, poems, plays

Characters and events in stories, etc., offer scope for musical illustration in a variety of ways. Ideas in this connection often arise spontaneously from something already going on in the classroom. One way is to make tunes to coincide with each appearance of a certain character.

For example, in one school where some first-year juniors were putting their own music to a dramatized story involving a witch and her wayward son, one child, who was learning the violin, insisted on playing a certain note as the most fitting sound for one of the characters. It was a difficult note to play in tune, but nothing could persuade her to use any other – she felt it best expressed her idea. Other children made use of various sized saucepans which they stirred or tapped with wooden spoons to illustrate a particular episode. Tunes for this purpose can be impromptu or worked out – remembered or recorded – metric or non-rhythmic. (A classic example of this is of course the story of 'Peter and the Wolf' musically illustrated by Prokofiev.)

The notes of the pentatonic scale certainly provide a useful framework within which children can make their first tunes, and their first ensemble music, but there may be times when there is need for other extraneous notes as, for instance, in making a tune for a mysterious interloper, an eerie cavern or an angular pattern. These might well call for the use of chromatic notes which belong neither to the pentatonic nor diatonic scale. These additional notes should therefore be available, especially when children become more advanced in this kind of improvising and composing.

As an extension to the making of simple illustrative tunes both tuned and untuned instruments can be combined to create background music or to evoke atmosphere for drama or dance. Again, there is no limit to what children can devise in this way and by the top of the primary school it can become quite a sophisticated form of expression.

Any situation which contains tension – mounting excitement or fear, an unexpected turn of events, extremes of feeling – lends itself very readily to this, e.g. a narrow escape; trapped underground; searching for treasure; the haunted house; a storm at sea; the unlucky magician. So also do general subjects such as Noah and the ark, a jungle, a funfair or a circus, each of which contains a variety of ideas.

3 Tunes to word patterns leading on to songs or instrumental music

When children are ready to leave the free improvisation stage and move on to using tuned percussion instruments for a particular purpose (such as making a tune for some words) it is generally considered simpler for them to begin by using only two notes. These are either G to E or C to A since they provide the sounds universally associated with calling. Using these notes, either on chime bars or on xylophones and glockenspiels (from which the other notes have been removed) children can make simple tunes to their names – first name, full name, names of brothers, sisters and relations, names of pets, etc. Several children can play their names one after the other and so link together these isolated sounds to make a musical phrase.

Certain everyday commands and questions are also based on these calling notes, e.g.

it's bedtime – wake up – supper's on the table – I'm busy – be careful – hurry or you'll be late – throw it – shut the door
what are you doing? who's there?
what's for dinner? where are you?
can you hear me? are you listening?
how much longer? are you ready?

Questions such as:

what is your name?
where are you going?
what are you doing?
what can you see/hear?

can be played by one child on one instrument and the answers played by other children on other instruments. This necessitates, as a minimum requirement, two sets of tuned instruments being available in one place at one time. Several sets are much better as more children can join in.

A list of nouns played on two notes very quickly exhausts melodic invention and is best considered as a preparation for further development. This can come about through the use of longer questions (see suggestions on pp. 31 and 32), but also by encouraging longer answers, e.g.

What is the time?
> The time at the moment is half past nine.
> The time by the hall clock is ten o'clock.
> It's time to go out for games.

Where does this train stop please?
> This train stops at East Croydon station.
> Passengers change there for London Bridge.

What did you see on your way to school?
> I saw the postman delivering letters.
> I saw a man mending a puncture.

How would you spend £1000?

Not only does this encourage more interesting tune making, but also the use of language. These longer sentences must also be given extra notes. The next to be used after G and E is usually the note A. Thereafter the other notes of the pentatonic scale are added one at a time, i.e. C and D and the upper octaves of these notes. In addition to extended questions and answers, tunes can be played to sayings and proverbs, repeated lines of poems, choruses, descriptive phrases, conversations, and original prose and poetry. The metric pattern of the words gives rhythmic shape to the tune. If, however, the words are later omitted, then an instrumental melody remains. Any of the word rhythms which are played on untuned percussion instruments can very easily be directly transferred to tuned instruments.

If a poem is given a tune so that it can become a song, and an accompaniment is required, provided the tune has been built out of the pentatonic scale any notes of that scale will fit in. An accompaniment should not have as many notes as the tune either in rhythm or pitch, and in fact, a single note played on the beat is adequate. Older children, however, may wish to experiment with more advanced forms. The setting of words to music and the making of instrumental pieces can expand to become a cantata or a miniature opera.

Occasionally a diffident child will find difficulty in transferring a word pattern to a tuned instrument especially when faced with two or three notes to choose from. In this case suggest: tap this pattern, on your hand, tap this pattern on your desk (one finger), tap this pattern on this chime bar. It is always worth while to help such a child.

3 Combining tunes – ensemble

To have composed one's own tunes is a very satisfying experience, but to participate with others in making harmony is even more rewarding – and this is where the use of the pentatonic scale pattern is of unique value for children. Tunes made from these notes can be freely combined without any fear of dissonance. Several can be played at the same time, provided always that the players listen to each other and keep to a communal pulse. This is closely akin to polyphonic music, a style much used by Bach and his immediate predecessors, wherein a number of individual melodies can be simultaneously played or sung while maintaining complete harmony.

Another approach is that of Carl Orff (see p. 33) where the three strands of drone, ostinati and melody are woven together. This in turn has an affinity with jazz in so far as in both instances individual improvisation is made over a set pattern of chording. The pleasure derived from this kind of ensemble is probably greater for the performer than for the listener, and this is one reason for its inclusion in primary-school music as it offers active and individual participation for many children. Musical interest and variety can be sustained by varying the rhythmic patterns which in turn alters the mood and character of the music.

Drone (usually the lowest pitched instrument)

notes C–G
(but these can be varied)   *etc.*

Ostinato 1

notes A–G–E   *etc.*

Ostinato 2

notes C–A–G–E *etc.*

Improvised melody

notes C–D–E–G–A–C–D–E

A further progression in ensemble playing involves the use of tunes made from the diatonic scale (i.e. C to C on a xylophone) combined with the chords I, V, and IV. Some reference to these will be found later in this chapter in the section on song accompaniment. Improvising with these resources however, requires a good deal more skill and a developed sense of harmony, but it can be achieved by older children who have had experience in these other forms of music making.

5 Pitch development

According to Dr Suzuki, the great Japanese educator, a child's sense of pitch can be firmly established if, from the moment he is born, he hears only accurately pitched musical sounds and hears them constantly. However, as these conditions do not obtain for the majority of children, the musical experience they receive at school must help them to acquire and develop this sense and also to make meaningful the terms 'high and low' 'up and down' as applied to musical sounds. Tuned percussion instruments are ideal for this because through their use each child can understand these ideas in a personal and practical way independent of their singing voice which may or may not be correctly pitched. They are able to integrate hearing, seeing and playing while they are learning to find:

next-door sounds (as heard on fire-engines);
ladder-like tunes (which go up or down one note at a time);
leaping tunes (which jump distances of several notes).

They can listen to the effect of combining various notes such as G and E, then G and A. Avoid predisposing their reactions by saying that some sounds are 'nicer' – there are few such absolutes in music – but rather encourage awareness of the difference.

6 Song accompaniment

Tuned percussion instruments cannot be used indiscriminately for accompanying songs since there is the matter of matching melodic and harmonic sounds. However, almost all nursery rhymes and many traditional and folk songs have a simple musical structure and this means they can often be harmonized by just two or three chords.* And these are perfectly possible on tuned percussion. Nowadays a great many of these songs are published with chord indications for guitar. These letter names, which form the bass note of the chord, can easily be transferred to the corresponding letter name on a chime bar or xylophone and this single note thus provides a simple but adequate accompaniment which children can play. These single notes can later be developed as families of chords. The three songs 'Michael Finnigin', 'Bobby Shaftoe' and 'The Little Red Wagon' all share the same harmonic pattern and therefore the same sequence of letter names can be used for each.

G
There was an old man called Michael

G
Finnigin

Bobby Shaftoe's

gone to sea

Jogging up and down in the

little red wagon

D
He grew whiskers

D
on his chin-i-gin

Silver buckles

on his knee

Jogging up and down in the

little red wagon

G
The wind came up and

G
blew them in-i-gin

He'll come back and

marry me

Jogging up and down in the

little red wagon

D
Poor old Michael

G
Finnigin

Bonny Bobby

Shaftoe

Won't you be my

darling?

* Two useful collections of songs which are suitable for infants and lower juniors and make use of common harmonies are *Tops and Tails* and *More Tops and Tails* by Anne Mendoza (Oxford University Press).

In the first place, children simply play their note of G and D when given a sign, e.g. You are my piano. When I use this hand (right hand), play the note G; when I use the other hand (left hand), play the note D. Watch and play, while we all sing the tune.

Since the letter names of notes are always inscribed on tuned percussion instruments, children soon begin to relate the sound of the note with its letter name and will very quickly be able to follow when these are written out on a chart on the blackboard.

G	G	D	D	G	G	D	G

For additional visual help at the start, write the letter D in a different colour, and also point to the letter at the moment the note is due to be played.

As a progression from the use of single bass notes, each note can have the other two notes of its chord added. This will then provide two complete chords for harmonizing.

One way of introducing chords to young children is to present them as being members of a family who share the family surname. The following chords are chords I and V in the key of G and can be constantly used, as many songs and most carols are in that key.

The 'G' family
Teacher plays and sings:

This is Mis-ter G

Here's his wife called B

Here's his son called D

G   B   D   make this fa-mi-ly

1st child plays and sings	I am Mr G
Other children respond:	He is Mr G
2nd child plays and sings:	I'm his wife called B
Other children respond:	She's his wife called B
3rd child:	I'm his son called D
Other children:	He's his son called D
Three children play their own chime bar and sing together	G–B–D, we're a family
Other children:	G–B–D, they're a family

The 'D' family
This is Mr D
Here's his wife F♯
Here's his daughter A
D–F♯–A, listen while we play.

Alternative words for older children:

G chord: The first note is called G
The next note is a B
The third one is a D
G–B–D, now we know the three

D chord: This chord starts on D
Then add an F♯
After that comes A
D–F♯–A, say and sing and play

The chart which indicated the single notes to be played can still be used, but the whole 'family' will play as one when they see the family name.

Children can also play these notes on xylophones and glockenspiels, but with these instruments it is less easy to have one child to a note. As an alternative, one child can play two of the notes and in some versions of the chord, one child can play all three notes.

Various forms of chord accompaniment

(*i*) played together on the main beat of the bar

(*ii*) 'spelled out' and played one after another beginning with the lowest
or highest note and in a simple rhythm to fit the song

(*iii*) played together, but in a repeated rhythmic pattern

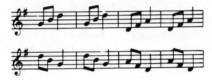

(*iv*) the chord split for 'um-cha' effect

As children become more experienced in these forms of accompaniment they will be able to devise other rhythms and to decide when a
rich or an economic texture of sound is the more appropriate.

The repertoire of songs which can be harmonized with three-chord
patterns is much more extensive, but the difficulty then arises of finding the best way to indicate the chord changes. The chart method is
still possible provided a method is found to show when the harmony
changes at mid-bar. Eventually it becomes clear that there is need for
written music either with guitar chord indications against the words,
or, as in some B B C pamphlets, with chord changes marked by different
coloured printing. There is another method which is used by Robert
Noble in his books *Folk-songs to Accompany* in which a special chording

code is used. This is possible in this particular context because he has collected songs which only use this restricted harmonic pattern. (There are three books in this series plus one consisting entirely of carols and they all contain very useful material indeed.)

The question then arises as to the extent to which this kind of accompaniment can be used. There is a limit, for as soon as there is a change of key or a modulation in the harmonic structure of a song, the three-chord pattern is no longer feasible and the accompaniment must be provided by piano or guitar. Moreover, there are only certain keys in which the chords I, V, and IV are practicable for most children and teachers. These are C, G and D.

The suggestion is sometimes made that children should be allowed to find the correct chords for harmonizing a tune by trial and error. This is certainly possible, although it depends at what stage they are asked to do this. For most children I have always found the process rather slow and not very satisfactory.

In spite of certain limitations, there is a good deal of benefit and enjoyment to be gained from making use of chords in this way so that children can accompany some of their singing through the use of tuned percussion instruments.

7 Notation of pitch

The use of tuned instruments is an invaluable asset in the understanding of pitch notation. It gives children a resource other than their voice (which is not always reliable) for the making of accurately pitched sounds and this gives meaning and impetus to the reading and writing of music and a way through to musical literacy which is interesting, individual and effective. Details of ways of linking pitch notation with the use of tuned percussion instruments are given in Chapter 8.

Some basic musical terms defined

1 A semi-tone is the nearest that two sounds can be to each other in western music.
2 A tone consists of two semitones.
3 A scale is a regular pattern of sounds built above a given note.

4 A chromatic scale consists of all the sounds there are, played in sequence, i.e. moving by semitones.

5 A diatonic major scale is a pattern made up of two tones and a semitone, followed by three tones and a semitone.

6 A pentatonic scale consists of five notes and omits the semitones of a diatonic scale. The notes of a pentatonic scale based on:

C are C–D–E–G–A

G   G–A–B–D–E

D   D–E–F♯–A–B

F   F–G–A–C–D

7 A chord is a matching combination of sounds extracted from a scale.

8 The lowest note of a chord is known as the bass (it also means base).

9 Chord I is so called because it is based on the 1st note of a scale. The third and fifth note of the same scale provide the other two notes of the chord.

10 Chord V is based on the fifth note of a scale and is built up, as for chord I, with the third and fifth note above the given note.

11 Chord IV is similarly formed above the fourth note of the scale.

12 A sharp makes a note a semitone higher and a flat makes a note a semitone lower.

13 In the pattern of the scale that begins on C there are no sharps or flats. Music using these notes is said to be in the key of C major.

14 In the scale that begins on G the correct tone and semitone pattern involves changing F to F sharp.

15 The first sharp is always F ('F for first'). It is always set out at the beginning of each stave, on the top line and applies to every F in the music.

16 All scales and chords follow a logical and immutable pattern.

17 Glissando is the rapid playing of a series of next-door notes. It can be done on a piano by using the back of the finger dragged across the keys, and on a xylophone by sliding the beater quickly across.

18 Body percussion is basically the use of stamping, clapping, thigh slapping, finger clicking, but it can include other sound producing movements of hands, arms and feet and vocal percussive sounds.

Chapter Three: Singing and Songs

> 'Since singing is so good a thing,
> I wish all men would learn to sing'
> William Byrd (1542–1623)

Given opportunity and the right kind of encouragement from an early age, singing can be a natural and spontaneous activity, but if left too late, a difficult and sometimes impossible pursuit.

There seems to have been a tendency of late to regard singing for its own sake as somewhat outmoded. This may be due partly to reaction by those who themselves were taught in a dull, unimaginative or over-didactic manner. It may also be due partly to the particular emphasis in primary schools at present on classroom instrumental techniques which is very right, proper and long overdue but which in many instances has developed at singing's expense. This is a pity. Both these aspects of music-making should be used to the full – they are comple-mentary to each other, not alternative options. The merit of singing is at least three-fold: it requires involvement at a very personal level; it is a corporate activity in a way that very little else is; it offers the double experience of using words and music.

For infants and lower juniors it is but an extension of speaking and the main aim is that they shall enjoy it and want to join in. It is almost certain at this stage that there will be those who are unable to pitch their voices to the correct sounds. This is immaterial to their enjoy-ment and on no account should they be discouraged from taking part, otherwise they will never improve. Ways of helping will be referred to later in the chapter.

During the junior stage, children should begin to be aware that their singing voice is a built-in, free musical instrument, always available, immediate in its response and with the same potential for development as any other instrument. It is here that many teachers and students lack confidence because they feel their own knowledge in this direction to be insufficient. But there is no need for this. It can easily be remedied once they have realized that singing is a practical subject and that the best way therefore to increase one's knowledge of it is to make practical experiments. So use your singing voice as often as possible: don't be put off by other people's comments: learn from observing all kinds of singers and persevere in trying out various ways of improving the sound. By these means, knowledge and self-confidence will be greatly increased. The inexperienced teacher will probably find it easier to begin by singing to younger children since they will not be critical and will respond at once if the right choice of song is made.

Since a song is nearly always a means of communication, it should be sung as such – simply, directly and convincingly – even if it is only a nursery rhyme. Remember always to look at children when singing to them and do not forget occasionally to smile. If it is a story song, then make it as ear-catching as if telling the story in speech. If the song is funny, make sure you enjoy the humour first so that it spills over to the children. If you feel you are not very good, practise privately to gain confidence. Make every occasion to sing an opportunity to improve. Watch singers and entertainers on television, particularly in close-ups – listen carefully to the sounds they produce and learn to compare them. Do not be content with what children achieve if you think they could do better, but be satisfied, for the time-being, if they have done their best, even if it is not as good as you would like it to be. Knowing when to accept a certain standard of music-making from children and when to try to excel it, requires very delicately balanced judgement. On one hand, there seems no reason for doing something in a poor or mediocre way when, with very little more effort, it could be done well – and there is always this choice. On the other hand, it is alarmingly easy to kill enjoyment by the wrong kind of insistence at the wrong time. Some teachers may remember having suffered in their own schooldays from the boring repetition of a few songs in order to reach the required standard for some special occasion. Consequently, they are naturally reluctant to impose anything of this nature on the children they now teach lest fun and enjoyment should disappear.

One sometimes hears the phrase: 'the children really enjoyed it – but it wasn't very good!', but perhaps if it had been good, they would have enjoyed it more; the one does not, perforce, cancel out the other.

To want to improve in any skill is both natural and necessary and is something which should be encouraged at all times.

The solution to the problem probably lies somewhere between the two extremes. It also depends very largely on the skill of the teacher concerned, the relationship between teacher and children, the teacher's sensitivity to children's reactions and finally, on experience.

An approach to singing

A good, lively singing session should be rather like a game of tennis where action and reaction are immediate, and teacher and children always on the alert with something more suggested and something more achieved. Spontaneity and improvisation are valuable assets in all teaching, not least in singing. The following comments are obviously not intended to be used all in one session, nor in every session, but occasionally, with discretion.

> Was that the best sound you could make?
> How about the mood of the song – did you feel it for yourself?
> What about the words – would someone outside the door be able to distinguish them?
> How about the sense of the words – are you thinking what they mean?
> Try to make your breath last a little longer.
> Think ahead as to what is coming.
> Were you listening all the time to what you were singing, or not?
> Do the words suggest how loudly or softly we should sing?
> Are some words more important than others? Speak them and find out.
> Is your singing better today than it was last week? (It should be!)
> Do you think it sounds well to 'bump' on the last note like this? (Demonstrate with slight exaggeration.)
> Always listen, listen, listen – to yourself and the others round you.

Gradually, the children will acquire aural and mental perception, discrimination and achievement, and a yardstick by which to measure and make their own assessments.

For the teacher's own development, much can be learned from the presentation of school music broadcasts on radio and television; from various festivals, from music advisers, summer schools, all kinds of courses – and always, from one's own vocal experiments.

PRACTICAL SUGGESTIONS

Learning a song

Children learn a tune more readily if it is sung to them than if it is played on an instrument. If the song tells a story, let them sometimes hear it right through (with or without accompaniment) so that they can absorb it as a whole idea.

The learning of words and tune together is strongly recommended as the one helps the other in establishing a tune shape, e.g. a certain word or syllable can be linked with a high/low/long note and this helps retain the sound in the memory as a peg on which to hang that part of the tune. 'Follow-the-leader' method is the most useful way because it is the quickest. Imitation is one of the basic forms of learning and advantage should be taken of this. If the learning process takes too long, interest wanes.

Try to detect mistakes quickly and then isolate them in order to put them right. They are usually the result of unfocused listening and can be rectified by making children aware of this reason. Sing with the ears as much as with the voice. *A repeated mistake soon becomes impossible to eradicate as it has then become a bad habit – it should be avoided at all costs.*

Listening, as opposed to hearing, requires the activity of the mind as well as the ear, and should be encouraged by any and every device. Concentration on what is to be heard is often improved by eliminating what is to be seen. Closed eyes assist close listening – but only make the children do this for a short space of time. To encourage attentive listening, suggest that after hearing a short phrase two or three times, any one or any group will be asked to sing it. (Remember to give a starting note.) It is usually wise policy to ask a group to sing rather than an individual, unless you know he or she is confident of getting it right. Children never seem to mind singing in twos or threes but can be

very self-conscious about doing it on their own and should never be
exposed to this until they are ready – it may put them off for life!

Certain intervals which cause difficulty can often quickly be set
right by drawing an enlarged pattern of the tune on the board. The
children can then draw it in the air while they sing it. (This is very
useful for seeing musical sequences, i.e. a repeated pattern of notes,
beginning each time on a different note.)

e.g. the 'spiral' of notes in the chorus of 'Ding dong merrily on high'

Glo   -   -   -   ria

or part of the song 'The Dashing White Sergeant'

Dance till dawn is | in the sky | What care you and | what care I

or the whole of the round 'Fie, nay, prithee John'.

Use sol-fa syllables, even if the children have only a small acquain-
tance with them, especially for the intervals of the chord which are so
often mis-learnt, e.g.

Immortal, invisible, God only wise

in this the notes on '–ble' and 'God' correspond to 'doh' and 'me'

Im - mortal, in - vi-si-ble, God on-ly   wise

la _____ [doh me] la _____

Correct rhythmic mistakes quickly by making the children clap the
pattern in imitation. Sometimes sing a tricky rhythmic phrase to silly
syllables – 'pom-di-pom' or 'ya-da-da', etc. Long notes can be instantly
and accurately sung by ticking off the required beats on the fingers,
e.g. the last 'alle { lu - - } ya' of the hymn, 'All creatures of
                   { 3 fingers }

our God and King'. It is the physical and visual realization of the rhythm that helps get it right.

Repetition is essential but it should be disguised. To make sure a phrase is well learnt, hear it sung by different groups of children – those at the front, at the back, those under ten years old, those over ten, only very very occasionally the boys and girls separately; hear it at various volumes – softly, loudly, whispered, getting louder or softer; at various speeds; on different degrees of the scale; with improvised nonsense syllables for quick passages; or in imitation of instrumental sounds; or whistled. Where rests occur in the music, click the fingers instead.

Have one group sing while another conducts, with everyone learning how to do this in 2, 3 and 4 time. Encourage a small wrist movement rather than a stiff, poker-arm one. (See diagram below.)

Begin here with
the right hand

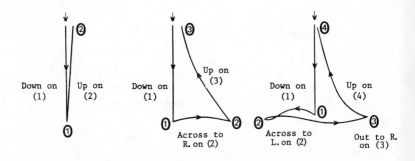

To find ways of circumventing difficulties is to prevent waste of time, effort and interest. It also gives a quick return in terms of achievement and this then becomes a stimulus for both teacher and children. Of course, many problems in learning a song resolve themselves if and when the children are experienced enough in reading music – although instrumental reading does not necessarily overlap into vocal. The ability to read music can and does happen in some junior schools, but it requires planned and consistent teaching over a number of years. However much we try to find short cuts, music is not an instant product, especially when it comes to using it in its written form.

The 'know-how' or technique of singing

I hesitate to use the word 'technique' lest it puts anyone off by suggesting something complicated and advanced or obscure and only for the so-called 'musical' ones.

This section is included, however, because so many times people have said to me, 'I just cannot sing' or 'I'd love to be able to sing, but I haven't got a voice', when what they really mean is that they do not know how to produce it. I am convinced that most people have a voice several times better than the one they make do with. They can discover this for themselves once they know a few of the basic facts involved in the mechanics of singing and if they are prepared to spend just a little time and perseverance in putting them into practice.

Although the following suggestions therefore are made for use at children's level, they are also intended to be of individual help to the teacher.

(a) Quality of sound

Ideally the tone should be warm, round and clear. This is the result of correct use of breath and production of vowel sounds, and many are the books and complicated the theories which try to explain how this is done. Obviously a primary school is not the place to propound these in any detail; on the other hand, as any development of singing as such depends on these few basic facts, some reference must be made to them.

Children are usually interested in the way their bodies work and at some stage it is worth spending a brief experimental session investigating how the lungs and ribs work, what resonance does to amplify sound, how air and sound cannot escape from behind clenched back teeth, how the jaw-bone is hinged and has uses other than assisting in eating, and that to sit or stand well not only facilitates breath control but is beneficial to health. To lounge over a desk or table is not conducive to good singing – even a BBC music broadcast has the occasional reminder to 'sit up'! You cannot swim with your feet on the ground and you cannot sing crumpled up.

Usually, when children are told to take a deep breath they immediately hunch their shoulders near their ears. To remain like that for only a few seconds is so incredibly uncomfortable that it proves it to be wrong. For really deep breathing, try to feel expansion in the lower part of the ribs, and pull in hard with the stomach muscles. To find if and how the diaphragm muscle is used in the breathing process, pant like a dog whilst keeping a hand on the midriff. Draw the breath in suddenly, as in surprise or fear, and then keep the ribs in that position while gently letting out the breath.

It is easy to take in a good breath, but not so easy to let it out in a controlled way; as the emission of the air is vital to the tone (cf. a recorder or organ pipe) it needs to be consciously checked. Breathe out on an audible 'sh-sh-sh' or 's-s-s', or 'h-aaaa' as 'h' opens the throat, in order to know that breath is being expelled with control and evenness. (Decide whether or not an appropriate image such as snakes or jets of water from a hose, is helpful – it usually is.) Vary the pressure of the escaping air, as this will eventually affect volume of sound.

Make some simple experiments in sound amplification through the use of resonators (e.g. a tuning fork). (I once heard an interesting broadcast in connection with this. A microphone was placed on the vocal cords and the sound amplified direct from there. This eliminated all resonance from the structural cavities of the head and face and the resulting sound was amazingly small – thin and metallic – rather like the voice of Donald Duck.) Finding the right place for the singing voice to resonate the maximum amount is very important.

Try humming with the lips just touching, then increase the breath pressure until vibration is felt in the lips and even in the nose. Repeat this with the lips apart making the sound 'ng' as in 'sing'. When this sensation is strongly felt in the front of the face, change imperceptibly from 'ng' to 'ah/u' as in 'cup' and try to feel it is being produced in the same place as the 'ng'. Eventually the sensation of all singing is felt here and it extends, with slight modification, over the whole compass of the voice. Some people do this naturally and others have to learn.

Faces and jaws which seem as rigid as if they had been in a refrigerator are not uncommon among English children, particularly those in the south, and this inhibits sound. Ways need to be found therefore to release these fixed positions. A yawn is often a good remedy. In this, the back teeth are well parted, the tongue kept flat and a wide cavity made in the throat – all of which are necessary for producing good vocal tone. Put the fingers on the place where the jaw-bone is hinged and feel the amount of movement there whilst yawning. This is to establish the right feel of movement for singing and is in fact where the formation of words begins. It ends with the nimble use of tongue, teeth and lips.

To do a wrong thing *once* can be the means of finding by contrast the converse and correct process – to try to sing with teeth clenched shows only too clearly what not to do!

(b) Clarity of words

This is governed by the sharp and precise use of consonants which although indispensable must never be obtrusive. All entertainers and most pop-singers are expert in this and on this score alone are worth studying. It can be both amusing and helpful to sing through a verse of a song omitting the consonants – to prove the point that the sense can only be understood when they are sounded. Whispering words is good practice and lip-reading also. Get a class or group to mouth a short message to you, as when the sound is off on the television – you may be surprised at what you read, and vice versa.

Aim to make final and initial consonants of two words collide, like cars riding bumper to bumper, e.g. 'come with me' = co ... mewi ... thme, 'and she would sing' = a ... ndshe ... wou ... dsing. With words such as 'lightly', sing 'ligh ... tly'. This gives long vowels and short consonants which is what is needed.

(c) Musical phrasing

This is simply musical punctuation and the making of intelligent musical sense. No one would think of ignoring commas and full stops in reading aloud or of stopping midway through a sentence, yet very often music is treated in this fashion. To be aware of musical sentences requires but a small amount of extra listening and thinking, and gives the whole thing coherent musical shape. Every phrase has a focal point, to and from which the music moves. Therefore the sound is seldom at one level of volume as if on a straight line, but graded, as in a curve or arch.

(d) Spirit or mood of song

Some might consider this to be the most important aspect of singing as without it, there is really no point in the song being sung. In a good song, the music inevitably expresses the spirit of the song – words and music are a marriage, not of convenience, but of compatibility. If, for instance, the music and words of songs such as 'The Dashing White Sergeant' and 'The Eriskay Love Lilt' were heard separately, there could be no doubt as to how they should be matched. To sing merely the words and notes, however, is to miss the raison d'être of a song and this is where imagination, sensitivity and awareness have unlimited scope. There is such a variety of experience to be understood, absorbed and expressed, especially in folk song, which fortunately at the moment is in vogue. It has always been worth using, however, and to enter into the inner feelings of a song such as 'High Germany' is to have shared an experience.

Obviously, to follow up all these suggestions would take considerable time, and they are not intended to be used *en bloc* in any situation. Neither are they to be rammed home at the expense of enjoyment. But it is possible (depending to some extent on the teacher's skill) to combine these two elements. It is hoped that the points mentioned be appraised, assimilated and then used with discretion as and when the need arises, each taking only a few seconds. It is not expected that the children's singing will suddenly assume professional qualities, but over a period of time an attitude will be instilled as to the worthwhile nature of singing and there could be a noticeable difference in the sound.

PROBLEMS IN SINGING

Unpitched voices

These are most apparent in very young children, especially among boys, but are also to be found throughout the whole age range. At the infant and lower junior stage there is no need in any way to draw attention to this discrepancy, but sometimes let everyone use their voice at varied pitches for non-singing purposes, e.g.

make your voice zoom skywards like a rocket;
make high, low, medium sound patterns – imagine their shape in the air – draw them;

imitate creatures with high- or low-pitched voices;
let your voice jump like a kangaroo, leap like a dolphin, and so on;
sing out of your feet – sing out of the top of your head.

This P E for the voice should help in finding the right feel of change from their usual limited compass of sound, when a next-door note is difficult to sing. It is always harder to distinguish between similar things, e.g. words like why, with, where and when, and much easier to grasp something very different, e.g. a word like hippopotamus. So it is with the adjustment of vocal sounds. Using the sort of exercises suggested above does not mean that non-pitched voices will immediately adapt – sometimes it happens gradually, sometimes suddenly – and there are times when one is defeated by a child's reluctance to try or to want to find the right sound. But encouragement, persuasion and the art of gentle insistence go a long way and eventually, maybe even after several years, the minor miracle may occur.

When, however, at a later stage these voices are still clearly noticeable and everyone becomes aware of them, especially in unaccompanied singing, it may be worth pointing out that this is just one of those things that happen, like some folk having straight hair or wearing glasses, and is something to accept without blame, to understand and to try to remedy. Children are very reasonable beings and will accept such explanation, provided there is a right relationship between you and them. It is best for a child with this problem always to be near someone with a strong sense of pitch and this should be arranged. For some it may help to play an instrument such as a recorder or chime bar. Alternatively it may mean then that they never try to do anything about their own voice. An inability to pitch may be something which has to be accepted, for a few children, but not many, are tone deaf (check by seeing if they can whistle in tune). Using the voice is such a personal and rewarding thing, that it is worth cultivating if possible.

High notes

This is a problem which usually exists only in the mind (especially of adults) since children's voices have a wide compass with the natural tessitura lying fairly high. It is a pity, however, for a song to be spoilt by a strangled-sounding top note for the want of a little knowledge to put it right. There are a few 'tricks of the trade' which may help.

It is essential when singing a high sound to allow the breath to flow freely and not to check it because of apprehensive anticipation. The mouth must be well open, especially at the back with as much space inside as can be managed but with no tightness or tension anywhere. Let the sound flow out without forcing. Imagine the note like a well-filled balloon, buoyantly floating up. A useful image is 'clearing the high jump – up and over'; placing the note on a high shelf, not from underneath, but from above; smiling and raising the eyebrows; thinking of the empty spaces in the head ringing with the sound; hearing the note in your head before you sing it. There are times when autosuggestion is sufficient, too many anatomical details confusing. Best of all is to demonstrate what you advocate!

CHOICE OF SONGS

Singing and songs are two sides of the same coin, and we come now to the all-important consideration of what to sing. One cannot always find something that matches up with the 'top of the pops' (indeed, some may not wish to) but the ingredients should be similar. If a song has a tune that sticks in your head, a rhythm that gets into your feet and words that are meaningful, it is well on the way to acceptance and enjoyment. This does not mean that one never sings songs outside these categories – certain songs in a minor mode become firm favourites – but as liveliness and activity are the characteristics of primary children's development, such music makes a very direct appeal. To find suitable songs may mean rummaging among many books since, in spite of the fact that there is now a great deal more available which is designed for primary school singing, it still needs some sifting and in the final selection it is a teacher's personal preference which decides.

For young children a song needs to be fairly short with an easily remembered tune and/or attractive rhythm. Songs with a simple chorus are good, especially when some of the children are not very nimble with managing words. Clapping is useful (e.g. in 'The animals went in two by two' – clap the 'hurrahs' and the last line) and a slight percussion accompaniment can enliven a performance. Be careful not to have too much or too complex an accompaniment as it can end up as a distraction. Some kind of action or movement is very necessary for young children and plenty of songs lend themselves to this. To sing and move simultaneously rarely seems to work, so either arrange it so that the two activities are done by alternating groups, or let them all move while you play or sing the song.

Words are sometimes a vexed point as they may belong to a period which makes them alien to present-day verbal style. I see no reason for automatically discarding a song because of this. It is possible for teacher or children to write other words – the BBC frequently resorts to this in its school music broadcasts in which good folk or traditional tunes are given a modern slant by using contemporary word idiom. Otherwise I have always found children perfectly able to understand that although the words may seem strange to us now, they were perfectly acceptable at the time they were written. After all, we tolerate the style of earlier periods in other things.

Until recently, folksongs have often been decried for a number of reasons, and an undiluted diet of them is not what is recommended. Yet many of them have the honest ring of genuine first-hand experience and are close to the grass-roots of society. The same can be said of sea songs and shanties, Negro spirituals, work songs and the true national songs of nearly every country. Many interesting links can be made between such songs and general topics for study.

The art-song form (Schubert, Brahms, etc.) is one which primary children are not usually ready to appreciate, and should be used with discrimination.

Modern songs are constantly on the market, as are various simple group cantatas specially designed for classroom use with opportunity for acting, for children's own accompaniment, and for improvisation. The choice and use of these depends very much on the teacher and the particular group of children concerned, but as they are so readily adaptable they are well worth using and should be included in any balanced repertoire.

There is a place too for the occasional cumulative and/or nonsense song to be sung just for fun.

With regard to using pop-songs and songs from current musicals in primary school, I can only give a personal opinion. To make use of something that is known and familiar as a starting point is sound teaching technique, but never to go beyond it, is not. Since the majority of children are surrounded by the sound of popular music from their birth, it could be a good and educative thing whilst they are in school to enable them to experience other aspects of music and other types of song. Also, as pop culture is acknowledged to be part of the adolescent development stage and musicals to be sophisticated adult entertainment, such songs would seem more suitable for inclusion at secondary level – except in certain circumstances when such an approach is the only way to gain children's interest because of antipathy or hostility to other kinds of song. (In such a situation it would probably be better temporarily to abandon singing as such in favour of the creative approach and exploration of sound so as to stimulate interest on a different wavelength and until a desire to sing was rekindled.) The constant use of these songs is often determined by the limited knowledge of any other suitable material on the part of the teacher (and in a few cases, by an unwillingness to find anything else) rather than a considered judgement as to their relative merit.

Rounds and part-singing

Most junior children thoroughly enjoy singing rounds which offer vocal harmonization with a minimum of difficulty in contrast to the usual unison line. There are numbers of books published containing a wide selection of these, but unless the original tune is one which can be fairly easily learnt and retained it is doubtful whether it is worth using. It is wiser never to attempt to sing a round in parts until at least the second occasion, by which time the tune will have had time to be absorbed and confirmed. With inexperienced teachers, rounds sometimes fail to sound well because there is lack of rhythm in the singing and no communal feeling of tempo. Ensure that whenever a round is learnt the rhythm is lively and accurate and the tempo consistent. It may help initially to tap or click the beat or to play essential notes on a pitched percussion instrument for this purpose. Also, decide and indicate the speed before you begin, to save having a false start. A satisfying effect is achieved if all the parts end simultaneously (each stopping at the end of a different line). The chording then becomes apparent and it saves the last group from having to sing their last line alone about which they sometimes feel self-conscious. Some top infants may be able to hold a part in very established tunes such as 'Frere Jacques',

'London's burning' and 'Row, row, row the boat', provided sufficient children have a reasonably developed sense of pitch, but generally speaking, the singing of rounds is something which comes more readily of its own accord from the age of 8 to 9 years onwards. Several collections are available which provide rounds of varying difficulty to suit the needs throughout a junior school. Some which are more advanced are 'All is Silent' and 'A wretched stupid fellow' (*A First Round Book*, by Kenneth Simpson – Novello), 'Fie, nay prithee John' and 'Summer is a-coming in'. These are quite demanding but very satisfying for older children to sing.

Just as there is a readiness for singing rounds, so there is a right time to sing in parts. It varies greatly with individual groups of children and is related to their innate singing ability, previous experience, stage of development, etc. Perhaps the easiest form of part-singing is to use a group to provide an 'ostinato' accompaniment to a song (i.e. a repeated pattern of simple notes which will fit throughout a tune). Some teachers (or children) may be able to make up their own, otherwise there is an increasing number of this type of song now being published.

The next step is probably the use of a tune above the original one, as in a descant. Junior children find it easier to sing above than below a tune and a descant to a hymn is one way of introducing this. It is short and it highlights a repeated tune. Always ensure that children who sing a descant, especially in an assembly, are confident of maintaining their part and able to pitch the first note unaided.. It is most demoralizing for it to go wrong and it is the responsibility of the teacher to see that this does not happen. It may eventually be possible for children in the top of a junior school to sing in two equal parts but only after considerably wide musical and singing experience. Where children are selected and trained to sing as a choir, then the possibilities for two-part work are further extended.

If there are competent recorder players in a group they can be used initially to play a second part. This helps in learning the music and in hearing the two parts together. When a lower voice part is needed, boys seem better able to cope with it than girls both in security of pitch and the timbre of the voice on low notes.

Thus, the art of singing and the repertoire of song, both individual and choral, can provide between them a source of ever-increasing pleasure and satisfaction – enough, in fact, to last a lifetime – and it is with this end in view combined with present pleasure that singing in the primary school should be taught happily and well.

Vocal improvisation

Even the most complex and elaborate developments in music have sprung from small and simple beginnings, and the art of vocal improvisation is no exception to this natural law. It does not begin with the sudden production of several long, well-balanced, varied melodic phrases. It begins, for most people, with the spontaneous singing of just three or four notes – and if this seems rather like speaking in words of one syllable, remember that this is how everyone first learned the art of using words.

Having sung two or four notes on the spur of the moment, it is really no more difficult to sing a sequence of five, six or eight, and very soon these few notes begin to grow into phrases or musical sentences. Here are a few suggestions as to ways and means of doing it.

Start with the simplest rhythm (i.e. all equal length notes), but as soon as more variety is needed, begin to change the rhythm here and there. Since the examples cannot be demonstrated vocally as they should be, they have had to be written out; and for convenience, all the notes are from the scale of C major. In actual practice, however, this is irrelevant.

(*i*) sing any two notes – repeat them – add a final note, e.g.

(*ii*) change the rhythm slightly, and use an extra note

(*iii*) make a 'return journey' of the tune, stay put, then –

repeat, and change the ending

C F E   D E F   G   C

To end a bar with the keynote (or 'home' note) gives a sense of completeness and finality. Conversely, to end on another note avoids this and gives the feeling of going on.

(iv)

(v) repeat a pattern by beginning it each time one note higher (or lower)

(vi) add a middle section by transferring the whole of the tune five notes higher

(a)

(b)

Repeat tune (a)

(vii) for simple rhythmic variation, change one of the crotchets in each bar into two quavers or into dotted-quaver-and-semiquaver

rearrange the rhythm into 6/8 time

So far, the notes of the tunes have only moved up or down a few at a time. There are two reasons for this. One is that this somewhat cautious approach can be of help to anyone unused to singing impromptu tunes, and the other is that similar basic patterns of notes are frequently the foundation of many folksong melodies. Awareness of this enables the range of tune vocabulary to be increased as these groups of notes can be linked together in various and individual ways to provide a further source of material for improvised singing.

Using once again the key of C major for the examples, these pattern groups are as follows:

(i) the 'calling' sound, i.e. as in 'cuckoo'

> G to E and C to A
> E to G   A to C

(ii) parts of a scale, i.e. a series of notes going up or down

> C–D–E–F–G / E–D–C / C'–B–A–G

(iii) a move to the next note above, and back

> G–A–G / E–F–E / C–D–C

(iv) parts of a chord pattern, either up or down

> C–E–G–C' / G–E–C / D–G–B

(v) repeated notes

Another approach is to sing a tune to words. Questions always make a good beginning. The need for an answer not only evokes spontaneous response, but straightway extends the tune.

(i)

What's the time?   two o' clock

What's the time?   five fif-teen

What's the time?   I don't know

What's the time?   Time to go home

(ii)

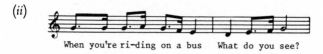

When you're ri—ding on a bus   What do you see?

Many short phrases in children's introductory reading books also provide ideal material.

Characters in a puppet play can sometimes be used as a way of introducing sung conversation as they seem to offset any strangeness that might exist in singing what is normally spoken. This difficulty, however, does not arise if children learn from a young age to accept singing as a natural alternative to speaking. Every day remarks can easily be sung instead of spoken, as can commands and comments. This can sometimes be applied to the telling of news items. With older children, the use of sung conversation can develop into the beginnings of opera – but let them use their own words and their own tunes.

Rondo form with its opportunity for individual improvisation between a set chorus tune offers another means of developing this skill. So also does the Orff ensemble principle of drone, ostinati and melody, as long as the notes which are sung conform to the pentatonic scale. (See chapter 2.)

Vocal improvisation is not necessarily a separate form of music-making. It can be used freely in dance and movement as a further means of expression. It can combine with instrumental work or it can take over from it, since most of what is played on tuned percussion, or recorders, can also be sung.

Children will only learn to develop this skill if in the first place the teacher has provided the initiative, and shown them the way. As with learning to speak, they will begin by imitating and end with improvising. Once again then, as with producing the voice, the onus is with the teacher to try things out. Experiment with humming, whistling or singing impromptu tunes – either freely, or based on these suggestions. Do it in odd moments – in the car, walking along the road, whilst working in the garden or doing household chores. In this way you will soon become competent and therefore confident – then the battle is won.

Chapter Four: Music and Movement

How music and movement first became linked together in man's development it is impossible to say – whether the rhythm of movement evoked a response in sound, or rhythmic sound the physical response – but linked indissolubly together they most certainly have been since the earliest times. There is perhaps no need to differentiate but rather to accept that there is a time for each approach, with the emphasis sometimes more on the music and sometimes more on the movement.

Both music and movement have certain elements in common and some which overlap, for just as music is a series of sound phrases, so dance is a squence of movement phrases – it is meaningless for either a note or a movement to exist in isolation.

In music	*In movement*
Timbre:	
quality of sound, i.e. 'colour' of variously produced sound and use of legato (smooth), staccato (detached), accent (emphasis), etc.	quality of movement, i.e. floating, gliding, dabbing, flicking, punching, slashing, etc.
Dynamics:	
change in volume – piano (quiet); forte (loud); crescendo (getting louder); diminuendo (getting quieter)	change in levels – high, medium, low; in size; in strength
Tempo:	
variety in speed – fast; slow; accelerando (getting quicker); rallentando (getting slow); pause	speed of travel – fast; slow; increasing; decreasing; pause

Phrasing:

the meaningful relationship of individual sounds – towards a climax, and away from it; the balancing of phrases by repetition and contrast; melodic and rhythmic shape	the meaningful relationship of individual movements – towards a climax, and away from it; the balancing of phrases by repetition and contrast; body shape/floor pattern/space pattern

This cross-fertilization between music and movement is beneficial to the development of each.

Moving to sounds

Young children respond very readily to the sound of lively, rhythmic music and are easily stimulated by it to move and to dance. There should, therefore, be some opportunity for them to do this. But it soon becomes apparent that the value of such movement response is limited by the children's lack of movement vocabulary and language. They need help in developing this and as with the initial stages of rhythmic and melodic improvisation, it will come about by a fair amount of directed teaching.

The voice

For movement itself – phrasing, rhythm, rise and fall, tension and release, etc. – the teacher's voice is an excellent instrument. It is a single sound that is clear yet variable and adaptable in pitch, speed, volume and mood and it can relate immediately to what the children are doing.

e.g.   begin by moving slowly,
        gradually get quicker and quicker,
        then stop!

Sound accompaniment (spoken, spoken/sung, sung)

      da - - - - - - - - - da - - - - - - - - - da - - - - - - - - -

         da - - - - da - - - - da - - - -

            da - da - - da - da - - da - da - - -

          da - didi da - didi – da - didi stop!

In this example the children's phrase is dictated by the teacher but as soon as the children have understood the idea they should experiment in their own time and their own way to make their own phrases, e.g.

repeat this several times, resting
as long as you like between each phrase
or
begin fast, then gradually slow down
to stop and use your voice to help you

It will be seen from these suggestions that any provided accompaniment could become a hindrance rather than a help in such a situation. In fact, it might well prevent a child from creating his own phrase and from developing at his own rate his own vocabulary. Children need freedom to explore and develop individually and independently ways of using their body in response to sound. This cannot happen with recorded music since it cannot follow a child's movements nor help to develop them. Therefore, in order that children may eventually be enabled to respond as fully as possible to the stimulus of music and to interpret it in movement, it is necessary to begin (whatever the age) at a relatively simple level regarding both the movement and the sound, and for this stage the use of percussion – vocal, body and instrumental – is invaluable.

Percussion

There are two ways of using percussion – the movement following the sound, or the sound following the movement. Children can move to the sound of a percussion instrument played by the teacher, by an individual child, by a group or, depending on circumstances, by each child in the class. As in the exploration and use of sounds in classroom ensemble or in sound pictures and patterns, both teacher and children should become increasingly aware of the intrinsic nature of each instrumental sound, but in this case with a different purpose in mind.

Remember that percussion instruments can frequently be played in a number of ways, each evoking a different movement response:

a tambour can be played
with a stick (big, strong, vigorous movements)

with the flat of the hand
with the knuckles (smaller movements)
with the finger-tips (light movements)
in the centre or on the edge
stroked with the palm of the hand (flexible or twisting
    movement)
with a marble rolled round inside (continuous shaping)
tapped on the rim with a stick (for moving parts of the body
    – hands, feet, fingers)

a single large cymbal can be
tapped with a drum stick or a padded stick for
    dramatic effect
played sharply and the vibration stopped with the
    fingers (for sudden effect)
played with repeated soft sounds
    increasing/decreasing sounds
    a wire brush (for small movements)
    on the edge with a stick

Whether the instruments used are orthodox orchestral percussion or the home-made variety, they fall into four main categories – instruments that shake, jingle, ring or are tapped, and these features should be fully explored and exploited. Eventually, the way in which an instrument is played and the particular quality of the instrumental sound itself will affect the type of movement response.

It would be ideal if every child in a class could have opportunity simultaneously to dance to and play an instrument freely but the practical problem of the ensuing noise prohibits this for most teachers except in very special circumstances. (Although it is worth remembering in this connection that most of the improvised percussion instruments have a very low volume level.) Alternatively, children can work satisfactorily in twos, threes or small groups, creating their own sound sequence to movement (and vice versa) using vocal sound, body percussion and percussion instruments.

e.g. in twos: one of you make a dance (i.e. a phrase or sequence of
    movement) while your partner watches carefully. Repeat it so
    that he/she can make a sound pattern for it.

or

> one of you play a pattern on your instrument – not too long, so that you can remember it – while your partner listens. Repeat it so that he/she can make a dance to it.

All this involves keen listening and the memorizing of sounds by both dancer and player and provides excellent aural training.

> or one child can make a percussion pattern while a group listens and then moves to it
>
> or a group can make the sound accompaniment for the class to dance to, and vice versa

This last suggestion offers considerable scope, especially for older children, as it can involve purposeful and careful music-making using both unpitched and pitched percussion and can be developed and perfected away from the movement lesson.

Be on guard against accompaniments of this kind becoming unintentionally faster.

When children dance to percussion in this way there must be repetition of phrase otherwise they cannot anticipate the next movement and the dance lacks symmetry, e.g.

bang – bang – bang – sha . . . . . . ke
bang – bang – bang – sha . . . . . . ke
rattle – rattle – rattle – g . . o . . n . . g

In all this improvisatory work, account must be taken, as in music, of how to conclude a sequence, for example, a climax and then a decrease, or an increase to a climax, or a natural ending of a phrase.

Moving to music

Moving to music

In helping a child to develop in terms of movement an understanding of phrase, sequence, rhythm, climax, etc., the introduction of music becomes necessary. It is good in the first place to choose music in which phrases are clearly defined and the instrumentation simple. The texture of much orchestral music is too complex for children properly to hear or to distinguish the underlying pattern, and in this context it is more suitable to use music with a single instrumental sound such as piano, guitar, wind, brass or for a small combination of instruments as in a duet, trio or quintet. The music should preferably be complete in itself and of short duration since children are being asked to listen in order to remember such things as the shape of the phrase, where it begins and ends, soft and loud sounds, legato, staccato effects, and so on. Certain piano pieces are very suitable for this (e.g. Schumann's piano pieces – *Kinderscenen*, Schubert Impromptus, Bartok's pieces for children or Beethoven's Bagatelles).

When children have had considerable experience in experimenting with movements ideas and have acquired a reasonable movement vocabulary, they can, after listening to such music, improvise to it. Knowing when to continue with one idea in order to develop it and when to discard it and try something else is a skill only gained by experience and it probably varies with every group of children, but it is a very important aspect of teaching. Progression from these beginning stages will depend on increasing the vocabulary of movement and on extending the duration of the music. In developing this aspect of movement, however, the improvisatory aspect should not be neglected but should continue alongside. The following examples are given to show how this kind of movement can develop with older children.

Dance sequence

Movement training required:

(*i*) galop steps – which foot leads; ability to travel and cover the ground

(*ii*) good, stable position for starting, arriving at end of phrase, and finishing

(*iii*) pattern across floor – curved, twisted, turned or straight; direction of travel; who do you meet

(*iv*) effort actions (i.e. push, pull, lift, drop)

push ⎫ with which part of body
and ⎬ in which direction
pull ⎭ at what strength

lift – high and light ⎫
drop – to low level ⎬ sudden or gradual

All these actions can be made strong, light, direct, slow, sudden.

Having had opportunity freely to develop these movements on their own, children then work out their own sequence using movement content only.

e.g. travel and travel and travel and arrive!
  push – push   pull – pull   lift – lift   and – – – drop!

Repeat this sequence four times.

After the 1st time   – arrive alone
           2nd time   – arrive and meet partner
           3rd time   – arrive in a group
           4th time   – arrive in a whole class

Sound accompaniment
The teacher can then accompany with rhythmic voice, drum or tambourine. The phrasing and metre must be clear and able to be anticipated. A progression from this is for a group of children to create their own accompaniment with voices or percussion instruments.

Dance to interpret a poem

It is important first to understand the essence of the poem, then extract the movement ideas from it. For example, a poem about an earthworm or a snake would lead to movement that was close to the ground, continuous, full of flexibility, curling and stretching. Body and group shapes would be smooth and sinuous. The accompaniment would keep with the phrasing of movement patterns and the continuity of body movement, and could be used to suggest a climax to the sequence. In this way, the music is an aid to the movement idea.

Dance to interpret music

For this, it is essential not to change the music pattern as children need to absorb and remember the sound in order to interpret it. The following points should be considered.

(i)   Starting position – whereabouts in the room; body shape; anticipation of next movement.

(ii) Melody – how it affects shape of movement or floor pattern. It is sometimes helpful to draw the melodic shape in the air with a finger or hand, then exaggerate the shape so that the body follows (i.e. draw with nose or forehead or elbow). Very clear patterns will emerge if the music is well chosen. A single instrumental sound is easier to hear and therefore to interpret.

(iii) Rhythm – which kind of stepping; use of clapping or other body percussion; feeling of travel; sway of body.

(iv) Social – alone, meeting, parting; with a partner; in a group.

(v) Finish – clear conclusion and stable finishing position.

There is a place for the use of more advanced orchestral sound when an atmosphere or mood is to be conveyed and this usually overlaps with dramatic interpretation.

To develop this is beyond the scope of this book but for those who wish to know more I suggest they read *Dance and Drama in Education* (Pergamon) and *Movement in Silence and Sound* (Bell) by Vi Bruce.

Singing games and activity songs

Although these are not strictly movement to music they should be referred to, as they involve songs with movement. Most singing games are rooted historically in the childhood stage of development and there is no doubt that they offer their own particular form of enjoyment at a certain age.

Similarly, activity songs such as those in *This Little Puffin: Finger Plays and Nursery Games* meet a very real need as far as young children are concerned, especially those who find difficulty with words. Young children benefit from singing songs which combine body, hand or finger movements and anything which enhances enjoyment should be used.

Traditional and folk dances

Again, the value of such dances is somewhat limited, but many primary children enjoy this activity and the tunes to such dances are unquestionably first-rate having survived the sifting processes of time.

Movement with music and music with movement are both an integral part of a primary school child's natural activity and so it should not be difficult to link them within the school situation. By the same token, to omit such activity altogether is to deprive children of both a source of pleasure and a source of development.

Chapter Five: Listening

This aspect of music in schools, is nearly always assumed to mean listening to records of music (usually orchestral) so that children shall become acquainted with this during their formative years in order to enjoy it more fully in later life. It would, of course, be foolish to deny that there is a place in primary schools for hearing some music of this kind, but at the same time there is the possibility of it having the same effect as having to read Shakespeare or Dickens at too early an age. Most orchestral music, particularly of the nineteenth century, is the result of specific and often sophisticated development and all of it is a vehicle of adult expression. This is not to say that children cannot enjoy or respond to some of it because music certainly has this unique capacity to communicate across all kinds of barriers and if the music is tuneful and rhythmic, it makes its own appeal on those terms. There is a need, however, to think carefully about what is involved both in the listening process and in the choice of music to be listened to.

No one can avoid hearing sounds but it is perfectly possible and increasingly common to avoid listening to them. Although to some extent this has always been true, it is only in recent years that, as a by-product of our age, children have been forced to develop this ability to close their ears as a self-defence mechanism against the relentless intrusion of noise. This in turn presents very real problems as far as listening to music is concerned, for in hearing more and more through the medium of radio, television and record player, they are listening to less and less. Listening, in contrast to hearing, is in any case a much more advanced process, considerably more abstract and involving a rather unique kind of activity that relies solely on the interaction of ear and mind. These things therefore need to be borne in mind when we ask children to listen to music.

When choosing something suitable for them to hear it is a good thing to introduce music that is gay, lively and rhythmic. Few children will be able to resist its attraction and unless the music they hear appeals to them, there is nothing to be gained by playing it. On hearing this kind of music, it is very likely that young children will want to move to it – to clap their hands, wave their arms about, tap their feet or move their bodies in a form of improvised dance which may or may not relate accurately to the rhythm – and so they should. So too should older children if they feel they want to, without shyness or embarrassment. Others may be content to be still. In either case they are reacting in a personal way to the stimulus of the music and the more freedom they have to do this, the better.

Music they hear may also stimulate some of them to draw or paint or model, or to write in poetry or prose. At all stages music has this power to act as a catalyst, releasing the imagination in an often remarkable way. In this context it is being used as a means to an end and not as an end in itself; even so, this can and should be one of its legitimate functions. Music chosen with this kind of response in mind is often evocative of a mood or an atmosphere as much as any pictorial representation and if it has a descriptive title, this need not be disclosed, or at least not until later. Such music makes an immediate impact and appeals very directly to such emotions as excitement, gaiety, mystery, fear, or aggression. The peculiarly distinctive sound of electronic music makes its own contribution in this respect, as it does for movement.

However, whilst most children can listen to music for these purposes without undue difficulty, they find it less easy to do so when the secondary motive is removed and the primary one is that of listening to the music for its own sake. They will be much helped in this if from the earliest stage they have been encouraged to listen to: (1) sounds around them, (2) their own music-making, and (3) live music provided by the teacher, other children or visiting musicians.

1 Sounds around

Listening to these is something that most teachers encourage when trying to develop awareness of the world through the use of the senses. Someone with keen hearing may notice a sound that others have missed and in drawing attention to it can help increase this aural alertness. For instance, every autumn a robin would sing outside our school hall but the children were unaware of it until we deliberately stopped to listen because they were so engrossed in making their own sounds of various kinds. Quiet sounds can easily be missed and noticing them needs careful cultivation.

Collect one new sound every day for a week.

Listen for soft small sounds from everyday life, e.g. rain on leaves or pavement or water, the changing patter of a dog's paws, 'clicking' in the radiator pipes, the whirr of a pigeon's wings, a letter dropped on the mat, dry autumn leaves being blown along, car wheels on a road that is wet.

Link this with a poem such as 'The Mouse in the Wainscot' by Ian Serraillier.

Collect other sounds that are: sharply defined/blurred; sudden/prolonged; similar/contrasted – in pitch, volume and speed; repetitive/irregular; that increase or decrease.

The finding and selecting of appropriate sounds for story illustration or for sound-pictures also helps in this development as it involves careful listening, comparing and discriminating. For example, a yoghurt carton tapped on the base and on the side does not produce the same sound; two identical-looking plastic containers may give differently pitched notes; flower pots have a variety of timbre and pitch; shakers filled with rice, peas, buttons, pebbles, marbles, screws, etc., offer a gamut of sounds within a limited range.

Consciously distinguishing between similar sounds assists children to focus their faculty of hearing more acutely and makes them better equipped to listen properly to the sounds of music, thereby enjoying it at something more than a superficial level.

2 Children's own music-making

Every time children make their own music, whether with voice or instruments, they should be developing this skill of listening. It is amazingly easy to be so preoccupied in producing musical sounds (especially on recorders) that we seldom truly hear them. Constant reminding and good-humoured insistence are necessary and then this awareness will gradually and surely grow. Whenever chording occurs as in rounds or in playing and singing in parts, there is opportunity consciously to listen. Even the sound of chime bars should occasionally be listened to simply for the quality of sound they make and for noticing that the same pitched note played on a different instrument gives a different effect or 'colour'. Sometimes it is useful to make a tape-recording of what is being performed, especially with group music-making, but this does not eliminate the importance of direct listening.

3 Live music provided by others

Primary children are very responsive to the experience of live musical performances whether by other children within the school, older children or visiting musicians. From the beginning of their school life they will have been accustomed to listening to the teacher as she sings the songs for them to learn, and as soon as individuals or groups of children can sing or play their own original music it is important that others should listen to it.

In this context, performing and listening are two sides of the same coin, to be accepted as natural and normal – not as an occasion for a few children to show off but something for all to share. Sometimes this situation can provide a direct link with recorded music, for having tried to make music themselves, children are more prepared to listen and understand someone else's composition, especially if there is a mutual theme. For example, after making their own sound picture of the sea and the life within it, trying to portray the restless movement of the waves, the sinuousness of seaweed, the unfolding beauty of sea anenomes, the scuttling of crabs, the movement and peculiar characteristics of various fish such as sharks, eels, dolphins, the darting shoals of tropical fish, the jet propulsion and slitheriness of octopus – it might be more meaningful then to listen to the sound-miniature of underwater life as portrayed by Saint-Saëns in the music of 'Aquarium' from the *Carnival of Animals*.

If it is possible to bring in older children from another school in the area who can play orchestral instruments reasonably competently, this will make a very strong and lasting impact. It is also good to invite local musicians with their more mature understanding of interpreting music, especially if they play less familiar instruments such as viola or bassoon, and ask them to include a short talk or demonstration of the instrument concerned. It is wise, however, to make clear beforehand that the talking needs to be brief and to the point, the music carefully chosen and within the listening span of the children concerned, otherwise more harm than good could result.

Development of true listening

When there has been much active participation in music-making at the children's own level and listening to live performances from others, a time should come for true, deliberate listening to music and for listening to the kind of music which cannot be produced in school but heard only through the medium of recording. When this moment arrives, there are certain factors to be kept in mind:

(a) that the listening span of young children is very short – two or three minutes for most infants

(b) this can only increase if there is continuity of approach between the age groups through the primary school

(c) the less complex the texture, the better it is for young children

(d) the music needs to have a direct appeal such as a clear tune and/or rhythm (as in most dances); a single instrument clearly to be heard and recognized (piano, guitar, violin, oboe, trumpet, etc.); a mood or atmosphere; a story, picture or programme; a link with a topic of interest (e.g. music from other countries or periods)

(e) the music must be heard often enough to become familiar

This last aspect is very important for it takes time to get to know music as it does to know people and from a practical standpoint it is easier to play music often if it lasts for only a few minutes each time.

The manner of presenting music for listening varies considerably. Some people suggest simply playing it through without comment allowing the children to absorb the sound, either consciously or subconsciously, and that this is all that is needed. This may be a suitable approach for some children or for a very small group but for most children, particularly those whose background and disposition make listening a difficult process for them, some external help or guidance is of benefit. To suggest something specific to listen for provides, in the early stages, a peg as it were on which to hang the listening until the music has become familiar. This might be a rhythmic pattern, an individual instrument, a loud and/or soft passage, the climax, a particular ending, fast or slow sections, the strong beat, a fragment of tune, the shape of a tune.

However, the talking must certainly never outdo the music, for in the end the music must speak for itself. (There is in all this, the sobering thought that between involved enjoyment and alienating boredom there is a very narrow dividing line indeed.)

The ability to listen and respond to music varies greatly between children, even within the same age group and from the same area. Therefore, the foregoing suggestions are but flexible guidelines, – offered, however, in the light of experience.

There is a practical point which arises from the present-day situation in which it is almost a reflex action to talk through or against music. In view of this current trend I have always found it worth saying that while it is not expected that everyone listening will be equally interested in the music they hear, it is expected that no one should spoil other people's enjoyment by talking or fidgeting. Children always seem very reasonable and responsive about this once it has been pointed out – much more so in fact than some adults.

Within a listening programme there is certainly a time and place for light-hearted music and the specially produced 'just-for-fun' record, but in the playing of current popular music, as with the singing of it, a little goes a long way. Apart from the fact that children are already perfectly familiar with it and conditioned by it, the pop idiom is but a very small fragment of music's many, many facets. There is a wealth of other kinds of music waiting to be heard, experienced and known. (I might point out in passing that it would surely seem a little odd if children's only encounter in school with the English language, for instance, was through the use of comics and magazines – yet, in terms of popular communication, these are the literary counterpart to 'pop'.)

As to the amount of modern music that should be played to children of this age, and at what stage this should be, opinions vary. Some hold that since much of it is in a neo-primitive idiom, it has very strong links with childhood itself and should on this account be introduced at an early age. The decision really hinges on the individual teacher's personal knowledge and preference in this direction and also on the time available. It would seem a pity from the children's point of view for any one aspect of music to be over-emphasized at the expense of another. Rather should their ears be opened to as comprehensive a selection of music as is suitable in the varying stages of their development so that by the end of primary school they have found for themselves how many fascinating and varied avenues music offers, each of which can tempt them to further exploration.

In the following list of suggested music for listening to on record, bear in mind that *only a small part of these records is suitable* (unless it already consists of a collection of short pieces), and there is no alternative for the teacher but to play the music through a few times and then decide which parts to use. I make no apology for including well-known favourites. Many of them have become so because they embody some of the qualities already mentioned, and there is some music which every child is entitled to know.

Selected list of recorded music

Sets of short pieces with strong melodic and/or rhythmic interest

Capriol Suite	Warlock
St Paul's Suite	Holst
Carnival of Animals	Saint-Saëns
Boutique Fantasque	Rossini
Holberg Suite	Grieg
Nutcracker Suite	Tchaikovsky
Façade	Walton
Peer Gynt Suite	Grieg
L'Arlesienne Suite	Bizet
Lieutenant Kije Suite	Prokofiev
Pulcinella Suite	Stravinsky
Hary Janos	Kodaly
Pictures at an Exhibition	Mussorgsky
The Planets	Holst
Jeux d'Enfants	Bizet
Prince of the Pagodas	Britten
Suite from *Carmen*	Bizet
For Children	Bartok
Kinderscenen	Schumann
Carnival	Schumann

Moments Musical	Schubert
Impromptus	Schubert
Scheherazade	Rimsky-Korsakov
Karelia Suite	Sibelius
Wand of Youth Suite	Elgar
Water Music	Handel
Fireworks Music	Handel

Single pieces

Waltz from *Eugene Onegin* and other waltzes	Tchaikovsky
Marche Joyeuse	Chabrier
Crown Imperial	Walton
New World Symphony (parts of)	Dvorak
Academic Festival Overture	Brahms
March from *Aida*	Verdi

Orchestral Music in Dance Form for lively rhythm and excitement

Norwegian Dances	Grieg
'Russian Dance' from *Nutcracker Suite*	Tchaikovsky
Slavonic Dances	Dvorak
Hungarian Dances	Brahms
English Dances (issued by English Folk Song and Dance Society)	
Polovtsian Dances from *Prince Igor*	Borodin
Espana	Chabrier
Capriccio Espagnol	Rimsky-Korsakov
Rhapsodie Espagnol	Ravel
Dances from the *Bartered Bride*	Smetana
Dance of the Tumblers	Rimsky-Korsakov
Polka from *Schwanda the Bagpiper*	Weingartner
Circus Polka	Stravinsky
Fancy Free	Bernstein
Ritual Fire Dance	de Falla
Sabre Dance	Khatchaturian

Stories

Coppelia	Delibes
Petrouchka	Stravinsky
Firebird	

Sorcerer's Apprentice	Dukas
Vltava	Smetana
Billy the Kid	Copland
La Fille Mal Gardée	Lanchbery

Atmosphere/mood (violent/peaceful)

Sinfonia Antarctica	Vaughan Williams
Nocturnes	Debussy
Coq d'or	Stravinsky
Rite of Spring	Stravinsky
Ride of the Valkryies	Wagner
Danse Macabre	Saint-Saëns
Night on a bare mountain	Mussorgsky
Checkmate	Bliss
'Sea Interludes' (*Peter Grimes*)	Britten
Music for strings, percussion and celeste	Bartok
Adagio for strings	Barber
Siegfied Idyll	Wagner
Clarinet concerto	Mozart
Introduction and allegro for harp, flute and strings	Ravel
Daphnis and Chloé	Ravel

Violin

Lark ascending	Vaughan Williams
Sonata in A for violin and piano) (last movement)	Franck
Violin concerto	Max Bruch
Violin concerto (last movement)	Sibelius

Miscellaneous

Symphony No. 82 'The Bear' (last movement)	Haydn
Surprise Symphony No. 94	Haydn
Simple Symphony	Britten
Classical Symphony	Prokofiev
Overture to *Ruslan and Ludmilla*	Glinka
Portsmouth Point	Walton

African music
Three sea shanties for wind quintet   Malcolm Arnold
Guitar music played by Segovia or John Williams
Listen, Move and Dance (EMI)
Court Dances of Mediaeval France (Turnabout)
Two Renaissance Bands (EMI)
Any David Munrow consorts

Chapter Six: Recorders

The sound of many recorders being played together may be far from the liking of the musical purist, but it can be a source of considerable satisfaction to anyone concerned with children's musical development.

The descant recorder's popularity as the ubiquitous instrument of the primary school is chiefly due to its convenient size and comparatively simple technique. Although it is frequently taught with the ulterior motive of enabling children to read music or of stimulating their interest towards playing a more sophisticated instrument, it must be unequivocally stated that a recorder is a musical instrument in its own right and should always be regarded as such. In spite of certain inherent limitations such as a rather small compass of notes and lack of dynamic contrast, it offers opportunity for the development of musical skill and sensitivity – especially when the several members of the recorder family are combined in ensemble.

Teaching the recorder

There are several alternative ways of doing this. A child may bring a recorder to school, having been given it as a birthday or Christmas present, and naturally wants to learn to play it – probably there and then, and in certain circumstances it may be possible for a teacher to find time and opportunity to give the individual help that is needed to do this. Or it sometimes happens that when there are several children wanting to learn, they are shown how to play certain unrelated notes and these are then incorporated into a particular song or piece of group music-making. Some teachers are in favour of allowing children to find out for themselves how to play the required notes. Charts are left about permanently which show diagrammatically the relationship between fingering and notes. There are children who manage to learn under these conditions, but more often than not such methods are inadequate in providing a sound and secure foundation that will enable a child to make steady progress and achieve musical self-sufficiency. Every musical instrument, however simple, demands certain playing skills and these skills have still to be taught. This may not seem to accord with some present-day approaches to other forms of learning in the primary school, but the method must be matched to the requirements of the subject concerned and there is no other way of learning to play a musical instrument well. All instrumental teaching, however, should benefit from the more enlightened attitudes which now prevail, so that the learning process is attractive and aligned to children's needs.

The paramount need of a child with a recorder in his hands is to play it, and this eagerness should not be dissipated or destroyed by unnecessarily long explanations. The quickest way to become proficient on an instrument is to use it, so make the instructions direct and relevant and as economically phrased as possible. This does not mean neglecting to put right what is wrong, and obviously care must be taken in the beginning stages to prevent the formation of bad instrumental habits and to foster good ones.

Let children learn to make their first musical sound on a recorder in the same way as they make their first word sounds – by imitating.

(i) All sigh – Haaaaaaaaaaaaa
    Sigh more slowly and make the sound last longer
    Make your sigh last for four clicks of my finger
    Do that four times – haa-aa-aa-aa haa-aa-aa-aa haa-aa-aa-aa
        haa-aa-aa-aa
    Now hold your recorder round the fat part at the top with two
        fingers and a thumb but do not cover any holes at all
    Sigh into your recorder
    Make four separate sighs
    Take your recorder away from your lips and whisper the sound
        of 't' very gently
    Whisper t-hoo-oo-oo-oo four times
    Now whisper t-hoo-oo-oo-oo into your recorder
(ii) Hold your recorder so that you can look through the hole at the
     back. Can you see right through?
    Cover the front hole with the first finger of your left hand like
     this so that you cannot see through to the other side

Now cover the back hole with the pad of your thumb
(Indicate left hand by saying 'the hand on the same side as the
window/door/playground, etc., to save time)
Press your finger and thumb firmly on the holes as though they
were trying to meet each other
Now sigh into the recorder
Change the sigh to 't-hoo-oo-oo-oo'
The sound we have played has a name – a letter name – it is
called B
Sing B–B–B–B
Play the sound of B four times

Alternate playing and singing – always. Beginning with the note B
on a descant recorder is both convenient and logical and almost all
recorder tutors endorse this. Also, when notation is later introduced,
the fact that B is on the middle line of the stave is a great asset in locat-
ing its position. But to play one note only for any length of time is
musically so dull that it should not continue for a moment longer than
necessary. Once the sound of B has been adequately produced, go on
next to the notes of A and G. These three notes provide the minimum
resource for playing a tune and the letters B–A–G form a useful
mnemonic for remembering the letter names. As soon as the relationship between the sound, the fingering and letter names of these three
notes has been firmly established, use them in simple improvised tunes.
The children watch, listen, then play by imitation. This increases
their visual and aural alertness and develops their musical memory.
They can then be encouraged to improvise for themselves.

Suggestions for ways of improvising

(*i*) By varying the rhythm, the style of the music is changed, e.g.
a slow tune

a tune that marches

a bouncy tune

a leisurely tune

a tune that weaves a spell (3 times over)

(*ii*) Use the word rhythms of well-known songs/poems, e.g. Here is
a new tune to 'Baa, baa, black sheep'

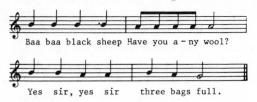

Which was the first word to have a different note?
Which word had the first long note?
Were the words 'yes, sir' 'yes sir' on the same notes or on dif-
ferent notes?
What were the notes? Sing them.
How many different notes for 'three bags full'?
What are their names?
How many fingers for those notes?

(*iii*) Use the idea of question and answer – sometimes with words
and sometimes without.

This kind of improvising lends itself to further development as
children can play their own tune in answer to the question and eventually everyone can learn to play the tune of the question. This is very
akin to rondo form in which there is a chorus part for everyone interspersed with individually improvised verses. Constantly alternate the

What's the time? Half past nine What's the time? Mid-night

2
or Which way shall I go? Straight a - long
Which finger shall I use? 2 2 2

or Which way shall I go? Down the road and back.
Which finger shall I use? 2 2 1 2 3

3
What are the notes you want us to play? B B A G
or Where shall we go for our walk to-day? *(improvised answer)*

playing of the notes with singing them to the letter names. Not only is this of benefit in learning the name of the notes but also in identifying pitch and learning to sight-sing.

Nearly all these examples which are based on the three notes B–A–G use only the 'one-at-a-time' finger pattern. It is important not to introduce the next step too soon nor to add more than one new idea at a time. Yet at the same time interest and enjoyment must be maintained. Try therefore to camouflage the consolidating process by varying the theme as in the above suggestions. Initially play only one or two bars at a time for this 'echo game', but gradually increase the length of phrase to be remembered. Always play each fragment *slowly and deliberately* to allow for each child to hear the tune, register it, remember it and reproduce it, and in the early stages give two or three chances for them to see and hear it.

Older children who are experienced players can still benefit from this approach by using it in a more advanced form, e.g.

(*a*) longer phrases;

(*b*) 'passing the tune' – one child improvises a short tune for another child to copy and then add his own tune for the next child to repeat the process and so on;

(c) play a short tune that the children play back with the notes in reverse order;

(d) play a short phrase which the children imitate using a different starting note, i.e. playing a sequence;

(e) state the name of the first note of a phrase then tell the children to close their eyes to that they memorize the phrase by sound only.

Some hints

Remember that:

(i)   there is no value in playing notes without listening to them:

(ii)   each child learns at a different rate and time must be allowed for individual understanding and co-ordination;

(iii)   anyone can play anything provided it is slow enough;

(iv)   it is easier for young children to put their fingers down than to lift them up;

(v)   each new finger movement, such as putting down or lifting up two fingers at once; needs separate teaching and practice;

(vi)   a finger pattern problem should be isolated and practised a few times without the notes being sounded;

(vii) children need constant reminders to sigh or breathe into the instrument (never to blow) and to begin each note with a gentle but firm 't-hoo';

(viii) the teacher should move around among the children while they are learning, giving individual help for individual difficulties, and not be tempted to stand at the front and assume that every child is coping;

(ix)   recorders can only be played loudly or softly by experienced players – otherwise all that happens is that the pitch is altered – contrasts must be made through variety of tonguing and phrasing;

(x)   one clear demonstration achieves more than many words of explanation;

(xi)   to say something once is no guarantee that children have heard or understood – to have them repeat it after you admits more chance of this.

Sequence of note order in teaching

Almost all recorder tutors recommend beginning with the notes B–A–G but diverge thereafter as to the best order in which to continue. Most proceed to the notes C and D because of the number of traditional tunes based on the five notes G to D which can then be played. Also because these notes are all produced by using the fingers of one hand only. Some children, however, are confused by the similarity of finger patterns for B, C and D and anything which can become a stumbling block to progress should if possible be avoided.

The more logical order of notes and fingering is to continue down the instrument by covering the next hole. Since, however, the next hole and the corresponding note of F provide the one exception to the general rule, it is bypassed and the notes E and D taught next. (This also means that the thumb of the right hand must then be placed in its correct position behind the fourth hole and the sooner it is taken away from helping to clutch the foot of the recorder, the better.) This then produces a pentatonic scale based on G and whereas this pattern of notes has not previously linked up with available printed music, there are now some books for young beginners which adopt this method (e.g. *Play and Sing*, books I and II, by Richard Addison published by Holmes McDougall). These books have the additional merit of using very clear, large type and of clarifying the reading of notation by changing the colour of each line of the stave as it is included. *Sing a tune, Play a tune* by Freda Dinn (Schott) and *Play Time*, Stages One, Two, Three, Margo Fagan (Longmans) also use this order. The particular advantages of this system of note order are that the recorder notes can readily be combined with tuned percussion instruments playing improvised ostinati as an accompaniment – which adds harmonic interest; it is a simple and easily remembered pattern of fingering; and it makes the playing of top E much easier as it can be taught immediately after low E and not as a complex move from top D.

The suggested order of notes thereafter is F sharp (as it is needed for all tunes in the key of G), top C and D, and lastly low F and low C. Low F has rather awkward finger co-ordination for young children but once it has been mastered then use the upper octave F straightaway.

At every stage of introducing something new it is essential to confirm what has gone before and if the necessary repetition is disguised in the form of various games, etc., sustained progress and interest will result.

Playing the recorder and reading the music

Opinions are divided as to whether it is better for children to learn to play all the notes first and to read them after that, or for them to learn notes and notation simultaneously. The latter method probably means that the playing of interesting tunes will be somewhat delayed since music-reading is a rather slow process. On the other hand, omitting to use orthodox notation means that children can never find out tunes for themselves but always have to rely on an intermediary person to transcribe the music for them. Bearing in mind that the sound always precedes the sign, the most satisfactory solution is probably to teach the playing of the sounds several notes ahead of the reading. This also gives opportunity for playing by ear, improvising and tune building.

The next choice is between the use of written letter names, e.g. G–G–A–B with a devised system for indicating rhythm, and orthodox notation on the stave. The use of letter names is similar to the use of i.t.a. in word reading whereby a simplified system helps to establish achievement and confidence. In both instances, however, the transition to the traditionally accepted forms of script has eventually to be made and if, in music, this is delayed for too long there can be a reluctance or even a resistance on the part of the children to this which can be quite difficult to overcome. This is because their ability to play new tunes is adversely affected and temporarily slowed down. Therefore it is better to dispense with the use of letter names as soon as possible to eliminate this kind of frustration. As mentioned elsewhere, whenever the stave is introduced it is essential to present it in a considerably enlarged form whether on chart, flannelgraph magnetic board or blackboard.

The teacher's responsibility

When teaching recorder to groups of children, always be very aware of those who are not managing to relate notes and fingering or who are simply following what their neighbour is doing. It is so easy to stand in front of a group or accompany on another instrument and be deluded into thinking that every child is playing correctly because the general effect sounds right.

Always give children an opportunity to say if they do not understand what to do or are lost – and always be prepared to believe them and give patient help. After all, children who want to play a musical instrument are not very likely to make mistakes intentionally, so if they are genuinely trying their best and still have not grasped what to do, it is the teacher's responsibility to understand this, analyse the reason and then try and remedy matters. This is a very important aspect of all instrumental teaching. It is only too easy for a child to be unable to cope, get behind and so lose interest and this need not happen if the teacher is sensitive to this situation.

Accompaniments and ensembles

In the early stages of learning, when the sound is still somewhat unpredictable, the use of a harmonic instrument such as the guitar, autoharp or piano can be of considerable advantage. Not only can it set the tempo and unify the playing, but it can help to establish that what is being done is indeed music – not just a series of dubious sounds. Some pieces, particularly those written in a more modern idiom such as *Fiesta* and *Beguine* by Brian Bonsor and *Alpine Suite* by Benjamin Britten, require the piano as an integral part of the music and essential in giving musical meaning to the recorder part.

But the individual timbre of the instrument is such that unaccompanied playing should always be cultivated both in unison and in parts. One consequence of this is that intonation benefits greatly. Another is that children learn to play together as one, in true ensemble. Children whose whole attention is engrossed in reading and playing cannot be expected also to watch a conductor and follow a beat, therefore it is more practical to convey the beat initially by a finger click. A sense of communal tempo develops surprisingly quickly and when this happens, the conducting – whatever its form – can gradually be dispensed with since the children will have learnt to play together by listening to each other, which is the essence of all chamber music.

When children have attained some proficiency and fluency in playing, let them use it in as many ways as possible – in assemblies, in songs, in classroom ensembles, with strings, in improvisation and creative work, and not least in groups where the recorder is played for its own sake and with the other members of its family.

Recorders and voices

Although the descant recorder has approximately the same range of notes as the voice (albeit an octave higher) and is often therefore given a vocal line to play, the unison blend of recorders and voices is not ideal. It is better if the recorders play through the song on their own, perhaps with guitar or autoharp or tuned percussion accompaniment and then play a different part with the singers such as an ostinato, a descant or a simple second part thus adding harmonic interest. Always make sure that the key in which a song is written does not contain too many notes which the recorder players have not yet learnt. The pamphlets which accompany the BBC music broadcasts provide excellent material for this approach.

Treble and tenor recorders

When the need arises for the more mellow sounds of the treble recorder, it is usual for some children to transfer to it from the descant. This involves learning a different set of fingering to produce the same notes and although this is competently dealt with by many children in junior schools, it can pose a problem for some. For this reason it is suggested that where instruments can be made available, a group of children whose hands have sufficient span could begin by learning the treble recorder and thus eliminate the difficulties of transferring from one instrument to another. Anyone who can play the descant can easily transfer to the tenor recorder when their hands are large enough to stretch the extra distance as the fingering and notes are the same. Usually there are a few such children at the top of a junior school who can cope with this, but because the tenor recorder is an expensive instrument, most schools reckon to have to provide it themselves and keep it as school property. It is, however, well worth the investment as it not only makes the recorder group musically more balanced but increases considerably the repertoire of music which can then be played.

There is a wide range of instruments now available produced by various makers and it is best to decide on one make and then try to persuade children all to have the same. Although a certain quality of production is now guaranteed by the British Standards Institution (the BSI kite mark denotes conformity with BSI standards), there is still a marked difference in quality of sound and a mixture of these various timbres adversely affects ensemble playing.

From experience I have found that the earliest age for most children to begin to learn a recorder is somewhere around seven years. A few children will be able to cope very well at a slightly younger age, but the co-ordination required for the fingering comes much more easily when they are a little older, especially for boys. To begin too early and find it too difficult can bring a sense of failure which is seldom overcome.

It is possible for young children to be taught quite competently by older children in a school provided the teacher has regular contact with the learners to make sure that not only are they playing the instrument correctly but that they are also understanding what they are doing and why, particularly regarding notation. It is also necessary to make sure that there are no personality difficulties between 'teacher' and 'taught'. This method may mean there is a chance of playing every day which is always preferable to having a lesson only once or twice a week.

Recorder teaching is sometimes undertaken by a willing teacher whose keenness to do it is not always matched by an equal knowledge of the instrument. In these circumstances it is important to learn to listen carefully to the sounds the children produce as regards quality and evenness of tone, intonation (i.e. playing in tune) and phrasing (i.e. only taking breaths where the musical sense requires it – not every few notes). Best of all, learn to play the instrument and if the reading of notation does not come easily, experiment with improvising.

Chapter Seven: Integration

True integration of music happens most easily and naturally within the infant school where it can be accepted into the whole curriculum. It can then be interspersed throughout the day in any of its aspects and correlated as and when it seems most suitable. Thereafter, the word integration tends to take on a slightly different meaning which implies only the way in which one subject merges into another. In this respect music would seem at first glance to relate most nearly to such subjects as movement (dance), drama and art. But there are other possibilities, particularly in the realm of children's creative music making, and suggestions for these can be found in the chapter on classroom instrumental music.

Further suggestions are listed below of more specific links between music and individual subjects. Some of them are more suitable for use with older children – top primary or even secondary – as they afford opportunity for quite extensive development.

English:
    as a stimulus to creative writing;
    use of language;
    original background music for poems, plays and dramatic situations;
    dramatic interpretations of music;
    the use of story and legend in music.

Science:
    how sound is produced;
    how sound travels;
    how sound is received.

Nature:
    music associated with the countryside, the seasons, birds, animals, insects, the sea, the elements.

History:
    songs and music linked with historical events, e.g. songs about Bonnie Prince Charlie, 'High Germany' (the press gang), 'Darby

Kelly' (the Duke of Wellington), 'Boney was a warrior' (Napoleon), Revolutionary study for piano by Chopin, *Fireworks Music* and *Water Music* by Handel;

music of various periods – mediaeval (early instruments), seventeenth century (madrigals), eighteenth century (dance suites), nineteenth century, (nationalism and romanticism) twentieth century (contemporary sounds).

Geography and other cultures:

international folk songs;

music from other countries by composers from France, Russia, America, Spain, Norway, Finland, England, etc.

Sociology:

development of people and conditions as reflected in folk song (rural and industrial);

minority groups (Negroes);

social conditions (sea shanties).

Art:

comparative development between art and architecture and music – e.g. baroque, classical, impressionist, contemporary, etc.;

paintings showing early musical instruments;

as a stimulus to children's painting.

Craft:

making simple instruments;

the development of particular instruments.

Religious Education:

all religious music;

Negro spirituals (use of Bible stories);

biblical musical instruments.

Dance:

as a stimulus for movement;

dance music of the centuries;

children's games.

Mathematics:

patterns, shapes and relationships.

Chapter Eight: The Written Language of Music

All the arts have the double function of being both a creative outlet and a shared experience. A child writes a poem, paints a picture or creates a dance and in so doing communicates directly its own feelings and intentions. What has been created in this way does not have to be repeated in order to ensure the communication – indeed, such repetition would more often than not be detrimental, if not impossible. But music, which is born in the imagination and creativity of a composer, has no life of its own until it is transmitted into sound by those who can read what the composer has written and only then does it become a living entity.

Whenever a musical composition needs to be given permanence, whether it be a child's simple tune or a highly complex work, then the use of notation is inevitable. This is not, of course, to deny the importance of improvisation, especially for children, but to clarify what sometimes seems confused thinking in this matter.

Therefore, although all the arts share certain characteristics, each has certain unique features and these should be recognized. It is often said that if a child can create its own pictures, it can create its own music. This is true and there are still too many children who do not have enough creative opportunity in music. But this resemblance is only partially true and we should consider rather more closely some of the unique features of music.

Between the conception of a musical composition in the mind of a composer and its eventual reception by the ear of the listener, the use of a written language (as in drama and poetry), has been necessary, an intermediary person or persons (as in dance and drama) and the extra-personal element of an instrument (as in an artist's paint and canvas) – and the first vital link in this chain of events is the ability to read what has been written.

It is the reading of this written language which seems to have been abandoned in many primary schools, either because in the past it has met with such little success or because it is considered to be inappropriate, unnecessary or too difficult. But need this be? It has not been thought inappropriate to teach the beginning stages of other languages in the primary school – English, French, mathematics, science – and the resources of music are of comparable value. It is now generally realized that to leave it until the secondary stage is too late. Children who have learnt to read music are equipped to participate both instrumentally and vocally in a far greater range of musical activity than those who have not, and with a much deeper sense of satisfaction and enjoyment. The reading of musical notation is certainly no more difficult than many other things which children cope with at primary school. Of course, it might well be that some teachers are daunted by what seems to them a difficult process and this is probably a reflection of their own unsuccessful experience of it whilst at school – an experience from which they may not have recovered. But the manner of presentation which caused this unhappy association need no longer obtain.

So often people say – 'I am not musical', 'I cannot read music' – as if the two things were synonymous. What they probably mean is: I think I am musical because I like music, but when I was young I was not fortunate enough to learn to read the language – and have felt handicapped ever since! This indicates yet again that it is time for something to be done.

There are those who feel that musical notation should only be taught as and when a child needs to record its own tune, and to some extent this is so – the need can certainly provide the initial impetus – but this haphazard method of approach is not adopted for any other form of language learning. Such an attitude means that a great many children will never come to terms with notation and the idea that music is only for a chosen few will be further perpetuated. Yet all great music educators such as Kodaly, Orff and Suzuki have been convinced that almost every child has musical potential but for the majority of children this lies dormant or even becomes atrophied because there is neither the opportunity nor the right teaching situation in which it can develop.

But perhaps the moment of change has come. Never before have conditions been so favourable for the successful learning of music's written language. In many primary schools there is now a flexibility of timetable that can allow for some music each day; there are musical instruments available in the form of xylophones, glockenspiels and chime bars which every school can in time afford, with a technique which every child can manage. There is also a great deal more knowledge and understanding of the processes of word reading which can apply equally to the reading of music. All that remains is to find enough teachers – class teachers – who are prepared to do this.

Comparison between verbal and musical development

Everyone in primary schools is very much aware that during recent years the two principal language subjects of English and mathematics have undergone some radical re-thinking and as a result there has been a tremendous change in outlook and approach in which most teachers have co-operated. Perhaps some of these newer attitudes could be of benefit to music where it shares with them certain aspects of language learning.

Just as children will have heard the sound of the spoken word from the moment they were born, so it is probably true to say that most children nowadays will have heard the sound of music of various kinds throughout their growing years. The difference is that whereas the words will have been experienced at first-hand as a means of ever-increasing individual communication requiring individual response, the music experienced at second-hand through radio, television and record-player, will not. There are, nevertheless, certain common elements.

In verbal development there are two aspects:

the oral – by which children are encouraged to talk freely, with flow, spontaneity and increasing vocabulary through the provision of stimulating situations and materials;

and the visual – in which graduated, systematic material is presented to enable the recognition, use and understanding of written speech.

Although the oral experience precedes the visual, they both develop alongside, albeit at differing rates.

It is very similar with musical development. Here the aural experience comes first, both at individual and corporate level, through singing, moving to sounds (vocal, percussion and instrumental) and the playing of musical instruments. It is essential that the pleasurable experiences of making music in these various ways should continue and progress while the visual aspect is introduced and developed. It is in the presentation of the visual aspect that many of the elements of word and music reading will be seen to overlap.

Basic approaches to word reading
  (*i*)   Meaningful sentence recognition
  (*ii*) 'Look-and-say' – for instant word recognition
  (*iii*) Phonics – for sounds of individual letters, diphthongs, etc.

Parallel approaches in music reading
  (*i*)   Meaningful use of known songs and music – for recognition of pitch through melodic patterns
  (*ii*) 'Look-say-and-play' – for instant recognition of rhythmic patterns
  (*iii*) Phonics/sonics – for names and sounds of individual notes, chord patterns, etc.
         (The system of learning the letter names of notes-on-the-lines and notes-in-the-spaces through the use of various mnemonics seems of as little relevance to music reading as the letter names of the alphabet were to word reading.)

Other factors which should be seriously considered are that word reading begins in the infant school; it happens every day; and the learning situation is left behind as soon as the foundations are securely laid – thereafter, children make use of what they know for their own pleasure and development.

As yet, this state of affairs does not apply to music-reading for, of course, it is not equated in importance with word reading, neither is there a comparable amount of material available, although the situation is improving. However, since the musical vocabulary is very much smaller, equivalent fluency can be gained more quickly – provided the conditions are the same. Since musical experience is a later development than verbal, it is suggested that the top year of the infant school is the best time for beginning such reading, although clues to notation could be introduced before that.

Conditions of music reading

Those who can read music have usually learnt to do so through learning to play an instrument, where the sound and the symbol were immediately and significantly related to each other. Also, there was opportunity to experience both aspects at frequent intervals – probably daily.

In the past, attempts to teach music reading to every child were hindered by the fact that the sound and the symbol were often divorced from each other or even taught in reverse order; that few children had a chance to make use of this knowledge in an individual and practical way; that progress was impossible with the recognition process happening only once a week or less; and finally, that there was little understanding of what is involved in visual adjustment when looking at music on a stave.

The first causes for lack of success have certainly been remedied in recent years, but the last one still presents a very real problem.

Everyone involved in teaching verbal or number reading knows that certain children find great difficulty in distinguishing between similar patterns of letters, words or figures. In music, the symbols used for indicating rhythmic variation are relatively easily recognized and remembered as they are simple, clear and contrasted. But the symbols denoting change of pitch are distinguishable from each other by only one thing and that is their position in very close proximity on the stave – which is of itself a visually confusing pattern of lines. Since almost all printed music makes use of a very small size stave, it is not surprising that some children never surmount the difficulty of reading from it. Whenever the stave is introduced, *it must be presented large, with widely spaced and very clearly defined lines* and only gradually reduced to the usual printed size. Of course there are always some children for whom these problems do not arise but, as every teacher knows, they are a minority group.

The final aim of all language teaching and learning is to gain competence in using it, according to individual ability and circumstance, and in order to try to achieve this it is necessary to present as many varied approaches as possible. The subsequent suggestions are made with this in mind, and also as a summary of the many ways that are available. Some of them can be used concurrently, e.g.

(*i*)   the use of word patterns with the use of French time names;
(*ii*) the understanding of pitch through melodic patterns with the use of melodic instruments.

Others may have to be selected and followed through as one system. All of them need continuity and constant revision if they are to achieve their aim.

Musical vocabulary

It is as well at this stage to set out the extent of musical vocabulary that a child could reasonably be expected to acquire by the end of primary school. The amount he needs that will enable him to read as much music as he will want to play or sing is relatively small (c.f. a word vocabulary of several thousand words).

There are five basic rhythmic patterns, from which eight other patterns are derived and twelve sounds of varying pitch, seven of which may on occasions be modified either up or down one degree. This is an intentionally limited vocabulary but one that is sufficient for primary school needs. If children can recognize these symbols and use them, they will be perfectly able to cope with anything new as and when it arises.

Pitch

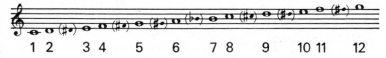

1 2   3 4   5   6   7 8   9   10 11   12

Rhythm

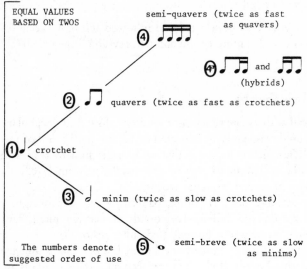

EQUAL VALUES
BASED ON TWOS

④ semi-quavers (twice as fast as quavers)

④ᵃ and (hybrids)

② quavers (twice as fast as crotchets)

① crotchet

③ minim (twice as slow as crotchets)

⑤ semi-breve (twice as slow as minims)

The numbers denote suggested order of use

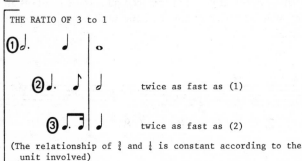

THE RATIO OF 3 to 1

①

② twice as fast as (1)

③ twice as fast as (2)

(The relationship of $\frac{3}{4}$ and $\frac{1}{4}$ is constant according to the unit involved)

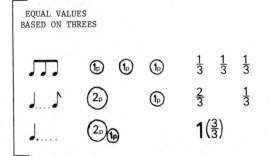

EQUAL VALUES
BASED ON THREES

①ₚ ①ₚ ①ₚ $\frac{1}{3}$ $\frac{1}{3}$ $\frac{1}{3}$

②ₚ   ①ₚ $\frac{2}{3}$ $\frac{1}{3}$

②ₚ①ₚ $1\left(\frac{3}{3}\right)$

The isolating of rhythmic and melodic development is necessary for the purpose of music reading, otherwise it is liable to become too complex and consequently a self-defeating procedure. The great need is for quick recognition and, as with word reading, once this is achieved, the children should use this acquired ability in playing and singing as much music as possible, for what they do not use, they will lose.

Most of this work should only be done for a few minutes at a time, therefore many of the suggestions should be considered as alternatives in providing the necessary repetition with a difference. Work cards and games for individual and group use are very valuable in reinforcing speed recognition but some of the ideas actually benefit from corporate participation.

METHODS OF APPROACH FOR THE READING OF NOTATION

Rhythm
1 Patterns of sound
2 Patterns of words
3 French time names
4 Counting the beats

Pitch
1 Patterns of melodic shapes
2 Use of tuned percussion instruments
3 Variable note shapes, coloured lines and notes
4 Letter names on the stave
5 Tonic sol-fa
6 Use of numbers denoting degrees of the scale
7 One line of the stave at a time
8 Recorders

RHYTHM

Since rhythmic pattern is in the very fabric of all music and all musical activity constantly involves its use, all that is needed in presenting the visual equivalent is consciously to draw on that experience and link the two together as directly as possible.

1 Patterns of sound

Children are very familiar with the idea of patterns in word reading, writing skill, mathematics, movement and art, and can quickly recognize rhythmic patterns in sound.

To prepare them for reading rhythmic notation it is imperative to give plenty of aural practice first, especially through the use of clapping and other body percussion. This not only develops their sense of rhythm, rhythmic vocabulary and focused listening, but is a source of enjoyment and fun.

Begin with simple patterns that everyone can do

Make them correspond to one bar's worth of beats

Progress gradually to more complicated patterns and longer phrases

Never do them for more than a few minutes at a time or stay too long with the same idea

Always have some of the aural patterns more advanced than the visual ones

Try to achieve a sense of progression

(i) Imitative clapping

Be my echo – when I stop, you start

or I'll throw you a pattern instead of a ball – throw it straight back to me

(clap) ♩ ♫♩ ♩ | ♩♫♫♩ | ♩ ♩ ♩ | ♩ ♩ ♩ | etc.

If unsure about being able to do this, start with the simplest pattern ♩ ♩ ♩ ♩ or ♩ ♩ ♩ and each time vary a different beat:

or think the word pattern of a line of a song, a poem, a proverb, a saying or an advertisement;

or clap the pattern of the words you might actually want to say – shut the door, open the window, tie up your shoe-laces, O – what's happened, go and fetch the milk crate.

(It soon becomes second nature!)

clap four crotchets

We've just made a pattern in sound. Here is its picture. This is what the pattern looks like when it is written out.

Clap it again while you look at it.

or: we have just been listening to the sound of Peter's feet as he walked across the room. This is what walking sounds look like when they are written down.

Sometimes notes sound as if they are running and then they look like this:

Sometimes they sound as if they are taking long strides and we draw them this way:

(To refer to walking, running and skipping tunes can be confusing because when children are asked to move to these rhythms they are just as likely, quite accurately, to skip or walk to all three. It is the sound of the music that walks, runs, skips, jumps, etc.) It is useful at this point to combine incidentally the sound of the French time names and some appropriate words, but only say them – do not write them.

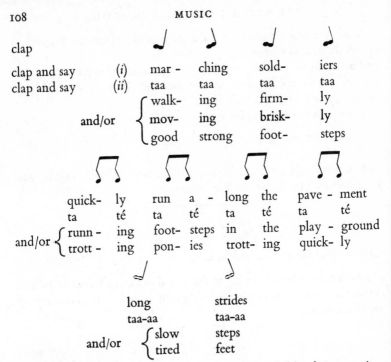

clap

clap and say	(*i*)	mar -	ching	sold-	iers
clap and say	(*ii*)	taa	taa	taa	taa
		walk-	ing	firm-	ly
and/or		mov-	ing	brisk-	ly
		good	strong	foot-	steps

		quick-	ly	run	a -	long	the	pave -	ment
		ta	té	ta	té	ta	té	ta	té
		runn -	ing	foot-	steps	in	the	play -	ground
and/or		trott -	ing	pon-	ies	trott-	ing	quick-	ly

	long	strides
	taa-aa	taa-aa
and/or	slow	steps
	tired	feet

Whatever approach is used it needs to catch the children's interest in a direct way. In this example the 'legs' can soon be straightened to give the correct form.

At some time the names of the note values should be gradually introduced, i.e. crotchets, quavers and minims. There is no reason to evade this, but as the only occasion for using these words will be in a musical context, children may take longer to learn and retain them.

1 Tell me when you think these sounds and shapes match (or do not match)
Display single flash card, then tap:

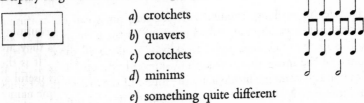

a) crotchets

b) quavers

c) crotchets

d) minims

e) something quite different

Initial success and confidence are important in the early stages, but gradually the differences can be less obvious and the matching less frequent, e.g.

2 Set out three cards as follows and number them for reference:

  a) tap one of the patterns and ask a child to select the matching card (eventually individual children can choose and clap the pattern when they are reasonably confident of getting it right).

  b) which card has the quickest notes?
     which card has the slowest notes?

  c) would you walk, run or stride to this pattern (show one card at a time and if necessary give initial help by clapping the pattern, but later dispense with this to encourage visual recognition only)

  d) I'll tap two of the patterns – which one has been left out?

  e) clap (or tap, or use an instrument) whichever pattern I point to (dodge about, but try to maintain continuity of pulse).

(ii) 'O'Grady' game
Aurally:

Clap patterns, one bar at a time, as in the echo game, but when the children hear a pre-decided pattern, e.g. ♩ ♩ ♩ ♩ they make no response. It helps to prevent mistakes if when they recognize the special pattern they fold arms or lock fingers instead. Be very sure that everyone knows the pattern to listen for.

(clap)

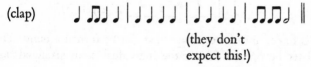

(they don't
expect this!)

Sometimes 'hide' the selected pattern by sounding it in some other way, e.g. finger clicks, arm slapping, foot tapping, etc. It is the sound that needs to be recognized, not the action. Vary the selected patterns *ad lib.*

Visually:
When children can recognize simple patterns visually from seeing them on individual cards, adapt the aural form of the O'Grady game to the visual approach:

> when you see the special (pre-arranged) pattern, do not clap it – we shall do something else there instead, e.g. slap your knees, nod your head, whisper 'taa taa taa taa', count out loud the number of notes, children with shakers (claves or jingles, etc.) play those notes on their own.

For this it is necessary to use a magnetic board, a flannelgraph, individual cards with temporary adhesive or a card that can be unfolded to show only one set of notes at a time.

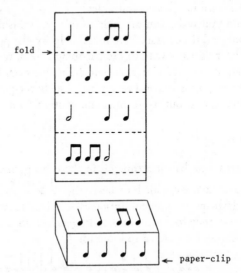

The card is folded into a box shape that can be turned around. The card can later be opened out or the individual cards arranged one under the other for sequential pattern practice using clapping, other body percussion or instruments. It is important initially to point to each group of notes to help children focus their eyes correctly and to ensure that no one has lost the place (which can very easily happen).

Additional practice suggestions

Using a card as in the diagram above:

a) I am going to clap one of the four patterns – which one is it? I will choose another and then you clap the one which is above (or below).

b) I will clap all the patterns through and make a mistake in one – try to spot it. Now clap that card correctly.

c) Two groups – A and B: group A clap all the patterns starting from the top while group B claps them starting from the bottom. (For this, arrange a signal for starting, e.g. after four 1 – 2 – 3 – 4 and keep a strong unifying beat.)

d) 'Mirror' patterns – as I point to a card, you play the pattern in reverse.

e) Sing the rhythmic patterns to 'pom' or French time names using two notes which can be pitched from chime bars or xylophone:

sing pattern 1 on the note E		♩ ♩ ♫ ♩
2	C	♩ ♩ ♩ ♩
3	E	♩ ♩ ♩
4	C	♫ ♫ ♩

Vary the sound by choosing any two notes, preferably from the pentatonic scale if they will later be combined.

f) All sing the special pattern ♩ ♩ ♩ ♩ on the note C four times while I sing (or play) what we have all just sung. Begin after four (3 – 4).

g) Two groups – A and B: group A sing that again and group B sing what I have just sung.

Here are your notes – group A   the note C
                                group B   the note E

Begin – now.

It is best to keep the sets of rhythmic patterns placed one under the other for some time as it is easier to recognize them as a unit, but at a later stage they can be set alongside as in actual notation for practice in reading from left to right.

Remember that – most of what is spoken can be sung and much of what is sung can be played, so there are endless variations to this theme.

(iii) *Imitative clapping used as a canon or two-part round*

Aurally:
Teacher claps slowly and deliberately
Children repeat the phrase

Teacher: This time, you start before I have finished, when I nod my head (or say now)

Teacher:
Children:

Teacher: Here is a longer pattern. Begin after I do (when I nod or say now) and try to clap all that I clap. Listen and watch very carefully.

Teacher:
Children:

At first, alternate a fairly patterned bar with a single long sound (be sure to swing the hands to indicate the silent beats in minims and semibreves, etc.) so that the next pattern is clearly audible. Gradually replace the single long note with minims/crotchets/mixed patterns. This is considerably more difficult and requires concentration and auditory discrimination and is more suitable for older children. Do not expect everyone to be able to do it straightaway, but it can be achieved and children enjoy it. This idea can also be adapted for use in singing improvisation.

Visually:

Using a type of card as in the diagram on page 109:

a) In two groups – group A clap through all four patterns beginning from the top; group B do the same but begin and end one card later.

b) In four groups – as above, with each group beginning one card later, as in a sung round.

Vary by using a different set of percussion instruments for each group, e.g.:

group A – claves
      B – jingles
      C – shakers
      D – plastic containers
         played as drums

This can give a complex and interesting sound texture.

(iv) Rondo form

This is the musical term for an extended 'sandwich' pattern which occurs in many songs – chorus – verse – chorus – verse – chorus, etc.

A – B – A – C – A

Aurally:

Using ♩ ♩ ♩ ♩ as the chorus pattern:

Children and
teacher clap: ♩ ♩ ♩ ♩

Teacher improvises
a different pattern: ♫♩ ♬♩

Children: ♩ ♩ ♩ ♩

Teacher: ♫♫ ♫ ♩

Children: ♩ ♩ ♩ ♩   (repeat)

This makes quite an extended piece of rhythmic sound. The 'verse' patterns can be given other timbre by using various percussion instruments as alternative to clapping.

At first, as with learning to talk, children learn these rhythmic patterns by imitation, but very quickly their own vocabulary becomes sufficient for individuals to be able to take over the teacher's part and this they should be encouraged to do.

Before introducing a new pattern visually, use it a few times aurally, e.g. as a remembered aural pattern for a rondo chorus

♩ ♫♩ ♩ │ ♩ ♫♩ ♩ │   so that the sound is being learned in

advance of the symbol and also with repetition.

Visually:
Using a card as in the diagram on page 109:

a) Clap the pattern of each card as a separate verse and intersperse a memorized pattern as the chorus.

b) Conversely – select one card as the chorus pattern for everyone to read and clap and then select three children to improvise alternating bars to provide the various verses.

As children become more skilled in this they will want to make a longer phrase – but it should not be of indefinite or indeterminate length. Making longer phrases also applies to the chorus motif and as there is a limit to aural memory the value of being able to read the patterns then becomes apparent.

A more advanced use of this idea is to have mixed rhythmic groupings, e.g.

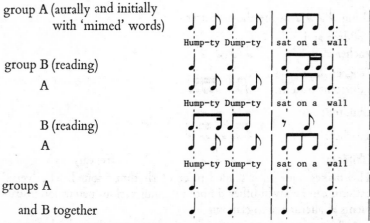

group A (aurally and initially with 'mimed' words)

Hump-ty Dump-ty | sat on a wall

group B (reading)

A

Hump-ty Dump-ty | sat on a wall

B (reading)

A

Hump-ty Dump-ty | sat on a wall

groups A

and B together

Similar cross-rhythms occur when combining the two rounds of 'Three Blind Mice' and 'Frère Jacques'.

Vary the chorus part by giving it a tune
Chorus (in its simplest version) and sung by rote.

Still use clapping or percussion instruments for the verses.

The tune began on the note G.

Someone work out on a xylophone what we have sung.

What are the names of the notes you have found out?

Let's sing the chorus to the note names instead of da-da-da,

e.g. G–A–G or G–A–G–A–G – G

When these sounds are written, they look like this:

If I cover up the letter names, can you still remember what to sing?

How many Gs were there – how many As?

Let's sing it again.

Progress from this to individual children improvising or composing rhythmic tunes – either vocally or instrumentally – as verses. (Play some music in rondo form, e.g. the last movement of Bach's violin concerto in E major or the 'Gipsy' rondo by Haydn.) It is not necessary to be limited to the pentatonic scale for this as only individual melodic lines are involved, not harmonic texture.

It has probably been noticeable that throughout these suggestions I have used only patterns with four beats in a bar and basically just four crotchets. This has been for the sake of clarity and continuity of example. Obviously other patterns should be used as soon as the children are ready for them and the basic idea adapted and modified to each new situation.

The use of the three-pulse pattern adds variety of metre, resource and of mood, but it is a fact that young children find groups of three less easy to deal with than groups of two and four, especially if they are asked to clap the first beat in a different way from the other two,

e.g. slap knees for first beat and clap hands for second and third beats.
The mimed movement of a blacksmith's hammer sometimes helps –
one strong aim and two lighter rebounds.

Rests in music
These have to be taken into account sooner or later – preferably sooner
– since they are an integral part of music's language, helping to phrase
and punctuate it. This is probably one of the few instances when a
brief explanation must suffice – for example, it is a note that has lost
its voice. In clapping patterns that include rests it is necessary still to
feel the beat without making a sound for it. Since there is no difference
percussively between ♩ and ♩ 𝄾, a way must be found for later
accuracy to differentiate between the movements. Having clapped
the notes, flap the hands in the air to indicate each rest. After a little
practice in using them imitatively they too can be written out for
visual recognition. The printed crotchet rest is, however, a very un-
manageable shape to draw so, as with the letter 'a', there are two forms.

♩ 𝄾 ♩ 𝄾   and   ♩ 𝄽 ♩ 𝄾

Bar lines
It is generally assumed that children understand the purpose of bar
lines, but very often this is not so. If they do not ask the meaning,
then tell them.

Early music was written without any bar lines but as soon as several
instruments or voices needed to play or sing together, the practical
need for visual guidelines become apparent. Their function is to divide
the music into visually convenient groups of equal beats – 3, 4, 5 or 12
as the case may be – with an implied stress on the first of each group.
They have no effect on the sound of the music other than where there
is an intended emphasis on the first beat as in some dance music or
marches.

Pattern of words

One of the ways of using words developed from the Carl Orff method
is for children to use the metric syllables of familiar words and names
and transfer them to a pitched percussion instrument. This means a
rhythmic tune can be improvised almost instantly and this is of great

value since it offers an immediate and practical way of making music. Children should be given every encouragement to do this. At the same time, it would seem but one step further to make use of the unrivalled asset of this rhythmic pattern in words to help children recognize rhythmic notation. The one slight drawback to using the spoken word in this way is that the inflection, and therefore the rhythm, of a word can vary according to how and why it is spoken. This does not affect the Orff approach where this aspect becomes an advantage in offering alternative rhythmic pattern.

In linking together a group of words for this purpose, anything and everything offers a starting point – a picture on the wall perhaps, or a topic such as the various forms of transport. The nearer to children's current interests, the better (e.g. steamship, aeroplane, train, wagon).

Aurally:
  a) Speak each word once, clearly and rhythmically.
  b) Speak each word twice to establish the sound of the rhythm and to make a balanced phrase.
  c) Repeat some of the words to give variety in dynamics and to make a climax, e.g.

  d) Speak and also clap every syllable of each word as in *(a)*.
  e) Speak each word first, then immediately clap the pattern of it:

  steamship ♩ ♩ aeroplane ♫♩ train ♩ wagon ♫♪
  (say)   (clap), etc.
  f) Mime the words while clapping the patterns.
  g) Think the words while clapping the patterns.

Visually:
The next time these are to be used (preferably the next day . . .)
have each word with its note equivalent written large on thin card
which will fold so that it can be used to show words or notes only as
required.

The following suggestions are not alternatives but need all to be
used on one occasion to help fix the relationship between sound and
image. This kind of sequence takes but a few moments to work
through and each step is intended to reduce dependence on the aid
which is familiar (i.e. the word) and to assist instant recognition of the
note which is unfamiliar.

a) Simultaneously read the words and clap the rhythmic pattern of
   the syllables:

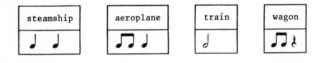

b) Read each word, then immediately read and clap the corresponding pattern (pointing to the notes helps to ensure reading rather
   than reciting):

c) Clap rhythm of notes and say words from memory.

d) Clap notes only.

e) Select any note pattern and ask for the word that matches.

f) Select any word and ask for clapped rhythm that matches.

Careful timing is needed to know how often one particular set of words should be repeated so that most children are sure but none has lost interest. Younger children very much enjoy the sound of repetition while older children, once they have understood, need the next stage introduced more quickly.

The collecting of words into topic groups and into rhythmic groups offers endless possibilities and can become as fascinating a pastime as crossword puzzles. Children should be encouraged to find their own word patterns and add them to an individual or a communal collection. With a class collection it is possible at any odd moment of the day for individuals, groups or everyone to clap through one set or another either across or down. Only by frequent revision will the sounds be thoroughly absorbed and remembered and reaction to the visual representation be instantaneous. And this is why this needs the interest and support of the class teacher.

The following lists indicate ways of using words for this purpose and also make the distinction between the manner of speaking the words. A decision needs to be made as to which kind of note shall be the basic musical unit – it does not matter unduly provided that whatever is decided upon operates throughout one set of words and the relationship between the note values is constant.

'Recited' rhythm	♩	♪ ♪	𝅝
	bread	cornflakes	soup
	milk	water	wine
	John	Andrew	Clare
	wren	bluetit	owl
	sage	foxglove	thyme
	York	Tonbridge	Crewe
'Natural' rhythm	♪	♫	♩

'Recited' rhythm	♪♪ ♪♪	♩ ♪♪	♪♪ ♩	♪♪ 𝄾
	maca roni	rice crispies	marmalade	butter
	Ara bella	–	Jonathan	Jenny
	oyster-catcher	king- fisher	humming-bird	cuckoo
	dande lion	bee orchid	shepherds purse	poppy
	Littlehampton	Peace haven	Aberdeen	Hassocks
'Natural' rhythm	♪♪♪♪	♪♪ ♪♪	♪♪♪♪	♪♪ 𝄾

The patterns already listed accommodate a great many words, but there are some other groups and these are set out below. Prefixes or unaccented syllables which are very common in English words are written as a single quaver placed immediately before a bar line so that the main accent of the word coincides with the main accent of the bar, i.e. the first beat.

One way of introducing several such examples might be as follows (the words are intentionally placed one below the other to show the use of the separate quaver):

♪	♩ ♪	e-normous
♪	♩. ♪♪	ri-diculous
♪	♩.	su-perb
♪♪	♪♪♪ 𝄾	hippo-potamus

The separate cards should then be placed alongside to show the usual order for continuity of reading:

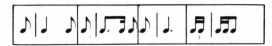

Finally the notes should be written with the separate quavers joined together as eventually happens in printed music:

Other examples

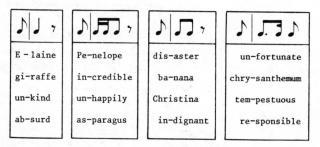

E – laine	Pe–nelope	dis–aster	un–fortunate
gi–raffe	in–credible	ba–nana	chry–santhemum
un–kind	un–happily	Christina	tem–pestuous
ab–surd	as–paragus	in–dignant	re–sponsible

When the words are read consecutively and there appears to be a slight gap in between, this gap is represented by a quaver rest ((ɤ)). If there is no gap between the words then a different rhythmic pattern has developed in which there are groups of three equal syllables:

These patterns of threes can then become groups of six equal syllables written in sets of threes, e.g.

varied as in

Benjamin Britten   Jeremy Thorpe

Most words that can be represented by  and can with a

slight change of emphasis sound as e.g.

Peacehaven Aberdeen  or
grasshopper butterfly

This nicety of emphasis can be used to demonstrate how the main beat in music can be equally sub-divided into two, three or four notes, e.g.

('recited' speech)

Manchester Birmingham   Tunbridge Wells

Edinburgh York   Bourton-on-the-Water

The grouping of equal syllables into threes and sixes is known as 6/8 time, in which a great deal of music is written, especially 'skipping' tunes as found in many nursery rhymes, e.g. Hickory dickory dock; O dear, what can the matter be?; Little Bo-peep; Humpty-Dumpty; Girls and boys come out to play; Pop goes the weasel; See-saw Marjorie Daw.

But although this rhythm is one that is very familiar to the youngest child, the reading of the several patterns involved necessitates real understanding of what is meant (except perhaps for those with a very quick ear and mind). It can be understood either through the word approach as already mentioned or as follows:

'Humpty-Dumpty' – in slow motion

twice as fast but still in groups of three

same speed, but in groups of sixes

The main difficulty that arises is that whereas in all previous patterns the crotchet has been associated with a one-beat value, here it represents two quick beats (quavers) and the adjustment in understanding has to be made.

There is one other main category of rhythmic pattern and this is the dotted note. Here the word equivalents are not so numerous. Short notes are meaningless until the next note is sounded and should therefore always be shown with the next beat attached. The effect of the dotted rhythm is more clearly heard when the words are spoken in the imperative or as an announcement, e.g.

the   world ... . at one!

Christopher!   go a - way!

Be - ware the bull!

Look out!   — it's   dangerous!

Sayings and proverbs
Aurally:
These provide word patterns for making longer phrases and again much can be done in experimenting with the manner of saying them, varying the inflections of the voice and thereby the rhythm. Rests of varying duration can also be introduced and this begins to give the pattern a better sense of phrase and also of contrast and climax. The

metric pattern can later become more relaxed and patterns of 5 and 7 introduced. A good deal of everyday speech fits into this latter category.

Visually:
The following short saying from 'Jack and the Beanstalk' can be used as the chorus pattern of a rondo:

> Fee, fi, fo, fum
> I smell the blood of an Englishman

Notation for it can then be introduced while still maintaining aural verse patterns, e.g.

When words and notes have been associated in this way a few times, then use the notes only.

Rounds
The months of the year offer suitable material for this approach and also include the prefix syllable (the weak beat which comes immediately before the bar line). This is a more advanced stage and would presuppose plenty of previous aural work.

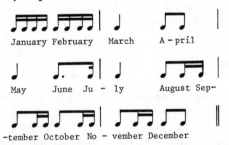

When children have had plenty of lively practice in combining the rhythmic pattern of words and music and in associating these familiar patterns with the written symbol, then the recognition process is accomplished and fluent rhythmic reading is achieved.

3 French time names

These were originally devised, as was tonic sol-fa, as a means of assisting music reading. The sounds were invented to represent accurately the duration of the various note values and these, once learnt, always applied. Unfortunately, they fell into educational disfavour for a time, partly because they were often presented as an end in themselves instead of a means to an end, and partly because it was sometimes found that the sounds for the more advanced rhythms were so difficult both to say and to remember that they defeated what they were trying to accomplish. (It could be of course that the English tongue is not as nimble as the French . . .) However, the sounds are logical and reliable and so there seems no valid reason for not making use of them, particularly in the primary school.

They can be introduced at the same time as the word pattern as an alternative, and taught alongside without separate explanation other than 'Here's another way of remembering the sound of these notes', e.g.

    (say)   nightingale   (clap) ♫ ♩

    (say)   ta-té taa   (clap) ♫ ♩

Rests in music, when taught through this system, need never be wrong It is eminently sensible to replace the initial 't' which begins the sound of each note value with an initial 's' instead and whisper the sound instead of speaking or singing it, e.g.

    ♩ taa   𝄽 saa

    𝅗𝅥 taa–aa   ▬ saa–aa

One other advantage of this initial 't' is that it is invaluable for articulation when playing the recorder and combines instrumental technique with rhythmic correctness.

There seems little to be gained as far as children are concerned in having the words for these sounds written out as they are essentially an aural aid, but for those who are uncertain of them, they are listed below. (The sound of té should be the short French vowel and not an anglicized version.)

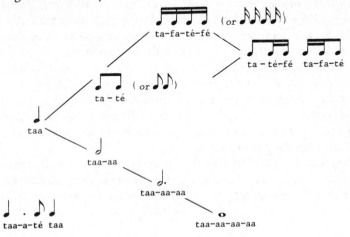

when this is properly pronounced it prevents the very common error of making this rhythm sound as ♩ ♪ ♩

this tends to become too cumbersome for actual use in quick 6/8 time but can be of help in the initial understanding of it

4 Counting the beats

This may appear to be a rather formal approach but there are times in ensemble playing when an inability to count correctly can sabotage the whole structure of the music. It is yet one more way of ensuring a secure rhythmic foundation and needs only occasionally to be used.

a) Instead of clapping the selected chorus pattern of a rondo, count aloud instead, e.g.

♩ ♫♩ ♩ | 1 2 3 4 | ♫♫♩ | 1 2 3 4

clap   count   clap   count
        aloud   aloud

Vary by making patterns in 3/4 and 6/8 time where the intermediary bars will need to be counted in groups of three or six.

b) Count aloud in groups of four but clap only on count one, then only on count two, etc. Vary by choosing a different beat in every bar, e.g.

⊘ ♩ ♩ ♩ | ♩ ⊘ ♩ ♩ | ♩ ♩ ⊘ ♩ | ♩ ♩ ♩ ⊘ |
1 2 3 4 | 1 2 3 4 | 1 2 3 4 | 1 2 3 4

Similarly, count in groups of varying numbers, for example, of fives, sixes, sevens, etc. and clap only on certain selected numbers:

1 ② 3 4 ⑤ | 1 ② 3 4 ⑤ | 1 ② . . . .

This requires a good deal of concentration and co-ordination. Counting the beats can occasionally also be used as an alternative to French time names:

(clap)	♩	♩	♩	♫	♫	♫	♩.	♩	♪	♪
(say)	taa	taa	taa	taté	taté	taté	taa–aa–aa	taa	saa	saa
(say)	1	2	3	1 and	2 and	3 and	1 2 3	1	2	3

This can sometimes clarify for some children the sound pattern

of   ♩. ♪♩

                          1 (2) and **3**

c) Orchestral counting – in any kind of ensemble playing which
makes use of a written score there are times when certain instruments or voices are not required to play or sing. This is shown
by a number which denotes silence for that number of bars and
the only way to time this interval correctly and to make an
accurate re-entry is by counting as follows – e.g. 4 bars rest in
4/4 time are counted:

1–2–3–4   2–2–3–4   3–2–3–4   4–2–3–4

The one other necessary piece of information here is knowing
how many beats per bar there are in the particular music being
played:

4 = 4 beats per bar
4 = crotchet beats

3 = 3 beats per bar
4 = crotchet beats

6 = 6 beats
8 = quaver beats

2 = 2 beats
2 = minim beats

Children always enjoy learning to count in this way and when they
understand how it is done they may well make use of it in their own
group compositions to lighten the texture or make a special effect.

I suggest that this approach be used last and then with discretion
since it involves more skills of co-ordination than the other ways but
it can sometimes fill in the gap which they may have left.

PITCH

1 Patterns of melodic shapes

Unlike rhythmic pattern which most children can quickly learn to
hear and recognize, melodic pattern is less easy to grasp and the con-

cept of sounds as high or low or of going up or down in pitch has little or no meaning for many young children – there is in fact no reason why it should. However, they will not usually find difficulty in making a high squeaky sound like a baby bird or a low, growling sound like a bear or of recognizing other extremes of pitch as between the top and bottom notes of a piano or guitar, but the nearer the sounds are to each other, the more help children will need to distinguish them. In fact, the convention of describing sounds as going up or down may have to be taught rather in the same way as the names of colours have to be.

The most relevant analogy in this respect is that of a tune going up and down stairs especially in view of the close link between the idea of steps and the musical term scale (*scala* – a ladder).

Introduction

Sing, whistle or play a fairly long pattern on one note.

Is this a tune?

Can you remember it easily?

Would you like to hear it often?

Why not?

Sing, whistle or play a series of notes up or down a scale.

How is this different?

Is the sound of this getting higher (or lower)?

If it is getting higher, we say it is going up – like an aeroplane or a lift.

Later, the up and down pattern can be slightly disguised by using notes that are not consecutive – for example, notes of the chord or every other note. Whenever a sequence of notes occurs in a song which illustrates this, use it, even if it is only two or three notes, e.g.

Baa baa black sheep – the tune to 'yes, sir, yes, sir, three bags full'
Humpty Dumpty – the tune to 'sat on a wall'

A very purpose-built example of a tune that clearly goes up and down in a step-wise fashion is 'Hickory, dickory, dock' but it should only be used in this way after it has been well learnt in its original form.

Meaningful use of a tune
A stair-case tune: 'Hickory, dickory, dock'

a) Sing the first two lines over to the children fairly slowly.
   Does the tune sound as if it is going up or down?

(Questions should always be framed so that in answering them children have a choice between two equally possible alternatives – more children respond this way and it avoids wasting time.)

   Having discovered that the tune goes up, establish this definitely by singing other words to the tune, e.g.

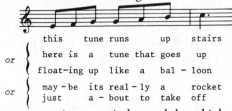

	this tune runs up stairs
or	here is a tune that goes up
	float-ing up like a bal - loon
or	may - be its real - ly a rocket
	just a - bout to take off

b) On the next occasion, recapitulate and then think about the third line – 'the clock struck one, the mouse ran down.' Listen carefully to the tune of this line (sing it without the words to 'dee' or 'pom' as words tend to camouflage the melodic outline). Here it is again – think about what shape it makes. Draw that shape in the air.

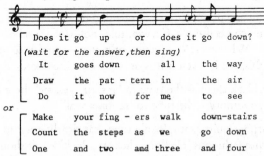

   Alternatively, sing the questions and instructions, e.g.

	Does it go up or does it go down?
	(wait for the answer, then sing)
	It goes down all the way
	Draw the pat - tern in the air
	Do it now for me to see
or	Make your fing - ers walk down-stairs
	Count the steps as we go down
	One and two and three and four

c) On another occasion, sing the last line of the song (also without the words) rather slowly and very distinctly, especially the first three notes. By this time some children may realize that the tune goes up first and then down.

The notes go up and then down as if they were on the steps of a ladder. Draw them like that (i.e. vertically)

Now draw them as if they were going up and down a hill (i.e. horizontally)

When each new melodic pattern has been discovered it should be recorded visually, either as a general outline shape or as a series of steps

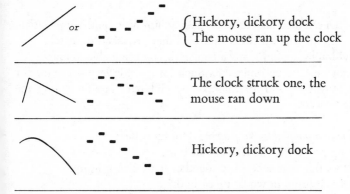

Finally, the patterns should be placed next to each other so that the relationship between them can be seen, although it is not always necessary to delineate the whole of a tune in this way.

The aim of such games is to help children recognize whole pattern shapes at a glance and relate them to tunes they know, which is what an experienced musician does all the time and what we all do in word reading.

As an extra visual aid make a simple cut-out man (basically a pin-man) and then move him up and down the steps while singing each line. Again, alternative but relevant words can be helpful, sung to the tune.

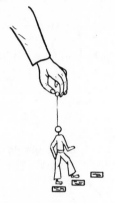

What will this little man do?
He's going to run up the stairs,
Now watch him slowly walk back down
Then quickly run down to the bottom.

Children can then take turns in making him walk on the appropriate 'stairs' according to which set of words they are asked to match.

Television has a unique advantage in this by being able to make each note light up as it becomes due. Such 'props' are very necessary for quite a long time and for maintaining children's interest during the learning process.

A tune with a jumping/spiky pattern: 'Hot cross buns'
    a) Sing or whistle the first line of tune.
        Does this tune take close-together steps or big jumps?
        Does it jump down or up or both?
        It begins high up, then jumps down low, then jumps back to the middle (demonstrate).
        Draw that shape in the air and instead of using the proper words sing 'high, low, middle'.
        (It is helpful always to exaggerate the distances of leaps when drawing the pattern in the air.)
    b) Sing the tune of 'one a penny . . .' to 'da' or 'pom', etc. . .
        Listen, think and decide how this tune moves and what pattern it makes.
        Draw it in the air.

Let's sing it to these words:
'run downstairs and then run back for
    high – low – middle'.

d) On the next occasion investigate what happens in the first part
of the next line – 'if you have no daughters'.
This tune is rather different – what do you notice about it?
Let's change these words. Sing 'it stays on the same note'.
The second part of the line 'then give them to your sons' has a
slightly more difficult melodic pattern for this stage and could
be temporarily overlooked but included in the sing through to
the alternative words, e.g.
'Let's stay on this note and then go off again
Run downstairs and then run back for high – low – middle'.

Draw pattern shapes in the air as often as possible and slightly overdo
any particular feature to be remembered – for example, very wide
distances for large intervals and deliberately small distances for step-at-a-
time patterns. When children have become aware through drawing
such patterns in the air that notes move up or down, that they can be
next-door sounds or widely separated ones, they will then be able to
recognize which tune it is by seeing the gestures only and will themselves be able to produce such matching patterns when asked to 'draw'
a song.

The pattern of 'Hot cross buns' can be given its visual form as
follows:

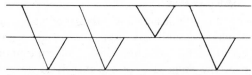

Sing the tune to 'zoom' and draw the shape in the air with
large movements while I point to it for you on the card.
Tracing the outline of this tune in the air rather resembles travelling
on a scenic railway at a fair – hence the use of 'zoom'.) Other relationships then become noticeable, e.g. each phrase begins from the same
place and three patterns are the same. Some children may make use
of this last idea as a way of extending their own tunes.

In transferring the general outline shape to individual 'steps' it is
wise to pencil in faintly a large size stave as in diagram (*i*) below, so

that the distances between the notes are accurately spaced, since the
relationship of distances between notes is all important. Later, the lines
can be filled in without necessarily drawing attention to them (see
diagram (ii)). Finally, the 'steps' can be changed into stepping stones
and be given the proper oval shape and the bar lines added (see diagram
(iii)).

(i)   (ii)

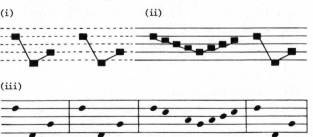

(iii)

At this point it may become apparent that there are varying numbers
of notes between the bar lines and this could be an opportunity to
introduce and combine the rhythmic notation. The moment for this,
however, is one for individual decision depending on the age and
ability of the children concerned. Some indication of note lengths can
be given in the 'step' stage by varying the actual length of the blocks
and/or their proximity to each other, e.g.

crotchets
quavers
minims

The combining of rhythmic notation with that of pitch is an additional
complication which should only happen when the separate understanding of each aspect is well established. Children cannot cope with
more than one new thing at once and they need time in which to
absorb each different idea. In this particular example, the rhythm
might first be indicated in the three bars which are alike and later in
the bar that is different.

All tunes are not quite as accommodating throughout as these particular two, although many nursery rhymes contain very convenient
pattern formations.

When using this approach with older children it is important to choose extracts from the songs they are currently singing, otherwise there is no meaningful link involved. Try to select for this a part of the tune which has a very clearly defined shape, to provide a musical landmark, such as wide leaps, next-door notes going up or down, fragments of tune which begin and end on the same note, etc. And these are not necessarily to be found in the first line. Gradually the extracts can include smaller intervals (i.e. distances between notes) and less striking and obvious patterns. Each song or hymn that children learn provides material for this, and each can have its own pitch-pattern picture. Just as children can tell from seeing an illustration in a story book which story it refers to, so they can learn to recognize a song by its 'picture' – and these can be collected together in a book for all to use.

Some examples

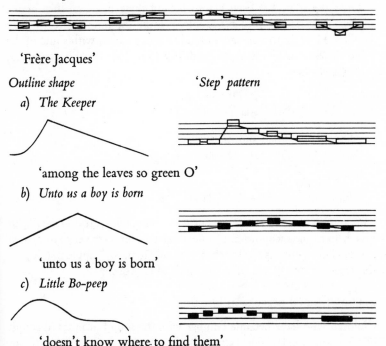

'Frère Jacques'

Outline shape   '*Step*' *pattern*

   a) *The Keeper*

'among the leaves so green O'

   b) *Unto us a boy is born*

'unto us a boy is born'

   c) *Little Bo-peep*

'doesn't know where to find them'

d)   The Dashing White Sergeant

'now the fiddler's ready let us all begin'

e)   The Old Woman and the Pedlar

'she went to market as I've heard say'

This musical digest of song quotations must be frequently referred to for recognition and reading and when a tune has been recognized (either from an outline shape, the series of steps or from the stave), sing it through to give the extra help needed by those who were unable to remember it.

Once the stave has been placed behind these patterns, then actual pitch is indicated. It is then possible, because the tune is already very familiar, to begin to associate individual letter names with some of the notes. These can be increased gradually to include the full range, e.g. 'Hot Cross Buns'

Sing: $D^{|}$ – D – G, $D^{|}$ – D – G
        la-la-la-la-la-la-la-la, $D^{|}$ – D – G

'The Old Woman and the Pedlar'
Sing: $D^{|}$ – $D^{|}$ – $D^{|}$ – D – D $D^{|}$ – $D^{|}$ – D

'The Keeper'
Sing: D – D – $D^{|}$ – A   la-la   E – D

This approach, however, is not entirely self-sufficient. It is primarily to give help in the recognition of tune shapes – a process very familiar to a musician – but, as with word reading, it needs supplementing at this stage by one of the other methods of approach.

2 Use of tuned percussion instruments

Children who have become familiar with the sound of notes (through playing tuned percussion instruments) and the names of notes (from seeing them inscribed thereon) are then ready to read the notes and there is in this approach a direct and meaningful relationship between the practical and the theoretical aspects. Notwithstanding, the problem still remains of the visual adjustment to the close narrow lines of the stave and since the essence of music reading is speedy recognition, everything should be done in these vital early stages to eliminate any possible source of confusion.

Because notation is linked here with the use of tuned percussion instruments, the order of the notes follows the order that pertains to the pentatonic scale. Therefore, in introducing the written notes of G and E, set each note separately on its own short stave as this is less confusing to children than seeing both notes on a long set of lines. An additional aid is to isolate the positioning of the note even more by indicating the inessential lines in a different way, such as by a broken line or in another colour.

the letter
name to be
written
inside the note,
above, below
or on the appropriate line

Notes are usually referred to as being in a space or on a line but it would really be more accurate to describe them as space notes and line notes since to a child 'on a line' often means something else, as in writing on a line. It can sometimes be of help to compare line notes with odd numbers and space notes with even numbers – both are needed to produce a consecutive pattern.

The next note in the usual order of teaching the pentatonic scale is A and this again should be presented separately. Thereafter, the three notes of G, E and A should be shown together in order that the relationship between them may be seen. Also, the break between the lines should be minimized, preparatory to being joined, e.g.

line   line   line   notes   tune shape line   space   line   notes   tune shape:

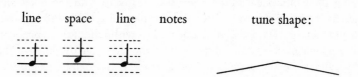

The note C is easier to recognize because it has its own line. It too can then be related to G and E which are all line notes.

line notes all the way   tune shape:

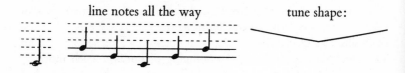

The note D should be shown in relation to the next-door notes of E and C:

related above and below

tune shape

Tune extracts using these notes for playing and/or singing:
  a) first two bars of 'Z Cars' theme

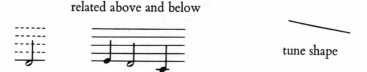

  b) first line of German carol 'Joseph dearest, Joseph mine'

  c) first line of 'O blow the man down'

d) opening bars of 'Morning' from *Peer Gynt* by Grieg

Further recognition practice can be gained at individual or group level by the use of simple work-cards, e.g.

a) sets of cards showing individual notes to be played as a game of 'snap';

b) short tunes based on each new note pattern for individual playing;

c) cards showing certain notes on the stave to be used as basis for children's improvisation;

d) cards showing individual notes to be used as flash cards for children to say – sing – play;

e) form of dominoes for the matching of end and beginning notes.

The preparation of these would involve time – more, perhaps, than many teachers might feel they could spare – but such aids would be of permanent value.

3 Variable note-shapes, coloured lines and notes

The beginning stages of this particular approach might be considered as 'clues to pitch notation' and be suitable for use with infants. Using the idea of 'shapes' with which children are familiar in other areas of learning, make two sets of differently coloured squares, for example, red and green. The red ones will be placed in the 'square' position and the green ones in a 'diamond' position. This is to make visually clear (*a*) the difference between line and space notes and (*b*) the similarity between all space notes and all line notes which at a later stage is very useful for the instant recognition of chord patterns. The shapes are basically the same because eventually they will all be placed in one position, i.e. as squares, which in turn will become steps, and then notes.

Arrange the squares and diamonds in patterns of alternating shapes:

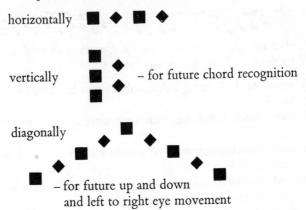

horizontally

vertically — for future chord recognition

diagonally

— for future up and down
and left to right eye movement

This 'play' with pattern shapes can be done by children in small groups who move the shapes around on a flat surface or in larger groups using some kind of adhesive device on an upright board.

The stave is then presented as a large gate (about 16 in. × 11 in.), preferably a cut-out one which can be handled and 'looked through' to check the number of spaces. Later it can be drawn on card with slightly longer lines to accommodate more notes.

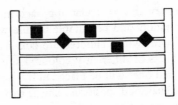

On one side of each shape write 'line' or 'space' according to the colours. The children then match these shapes appropriately onto the stave and move them about in various ways, e.g.

a) make a row of shapes in the same space/on the same line;
b) move them to another space/line;
c) put the line shapes one underneath each other on next-door lines;
d) put them on next-door lines but spread them out – make them go up/down;
e) put a shape on every line and in every space.

This individual handling and placing of the shapes helps children consciously to locate the various lines and spaces and become more aware of them.

Here is the pattern of part of a song you know (have it written out on a card).

Can you put your shapes in the same places?

Later the children may be able to remember the placing without reference to the card.

'Frère Jacques'

'Three blind mice'

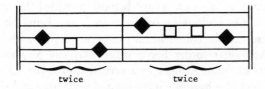

When this idea has been grasped, all the shapes can then be placed on the stave in the same square position, but still keeping the two colours to distinguish line and space notes (see diagram (i)). The next step is to make the colour uniform as shown in diagram (ii) and finally to turn the shape into a 'stepping stone' or normal shape note, as in diagram (iii).

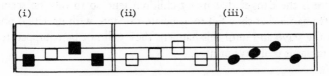

The letter names can be introduced either one at a time as needed or through this process of matching. On the large 'gate-like' stave, write the letter names of the space notes down one 'gate-post' and those of the line notes down the other. Write the corresponding letter names on the red and green shapes and they can then be matched and placed in position.

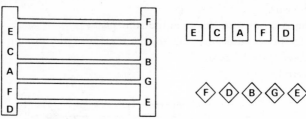

Always begin with a limited number and link with a familiar tune, e.g.
'Frère Jacques'   G–A–B–G
'Three blind mice'   B–A–G

Coloured lines and notes
There is a system of using a different colour for each line of the stave and/or each note. This can prove helpful, provided that at the same time the various positioning of the notes is also being observed and registered so that the colour factor can eventually be withdrawn. The Richard Addison recorder books called *Play and Sing* make use of this process of coloured lines to a certain degree (see Chapter 6 on recorders) and also have the stave printed very large and clear which is a great advantage.

4 Letter names on the stave

This is a useful shorthand method for presenting pitch notation and one that many teachers adopt. It is also the basis for the 'instant music' approach favoured by Rolf Harris. In using this for too long, however, there is the danger that many children tend so to rely on seeing the letter name that they fail to associate the note with its actual position on the stave and until this happens they will not be equipped to read music as it is always printed.

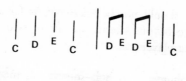

5 Tonic sol-fa

This was developed as an aid to sight-singing and as such is of undisputed value. As with the French time names (with which it shares a basically aural approach), it too has suffered a temporary eclipse in the realm of educational music because of unfortunate or inadequate presentation. Nevertheless, there is nothing wrong with its substance and it is now re-emerging as a worthwhile and reliable method. It demonstrates how the relationship between the sound of individual notes is constant whatever the starting note may be. This advantage is particularly noticeable in appreciating the relationships of notes in chord patterns. The learning of the singing-names of sol-fa is approached a few notes at a time and nowadays is often linked with the use of the pentatonic scale in instrumental development, e.g.

play G – E	sing soh – me
G – A – G	soh – la – soh
G – E – C	soh – me – doh
E – D – C	me – ray – doh

In making the transfer to the stave of these tonic sol-fa patterns, it becomes essential to locate the position of doh (or the key-note) and this highlights one of the disadvantages of this approach for although it does not matter aurally when the position of doh changes, it matters visually, and involves knowing about keys, key signatures, sharps and flats, etc. For many people this is one of the most off-putting aspects of music and certainly it is one of the last to be introduced into primary school work. It should not be necessary, as far as music reading is concerned, to go beyond the use of one or two sharps and one flat (except for string players).

Each of these four note patterns can provide very useful ingredients for tune-making and many folk songs are based on such pattern units (see vocal improvisation), e.g.

The explanation of the reason for using sharps and flats is that they are needed to maintain the same pattern of sound as provided by the scale of C. A scale which begins on G requires the F to be changed of F sharp and the scale which begins on F needs the B changed to B flat.

6 Use of numbers denoting degrees of the scale

This again is a logical approach soundly based on the musical practice to referring to distances between notes as thirds or fifths or octaves, etc., and since there are but seven letters or degrees in the musical alphabet (because the eighth one matches in name and sound), it has the attraction of a package deal in terms of the amount to be learnt. It shares with tonic sol-fa the constancy of relationship between the notes of the scale together with the use of the whole scale and of making the key-note (or doh) the starting point. Visually it has much to commend it. In the initial stages, however, it would not appear to have the meaningful connection with other aspects of children's music-making and therefore the gradual building up of the range of notes from 1–2–3 . . . onwards tends to occur simply as a learning process, somewhat akin to an entirely phonic approach in word reading. Again, the visual realization of chord patterns is clarified and this is valuable for knowing how to build chords for use with chime bars and for understanding chord terminology for accompaniments – chords I, V, IV, etc.

7 One line of the stave at a time

To begin music reading by starting with only one line of the stave has very close connection with the historical development of notation itself. When tunes first needed recording in written form the melodic outline was approximately preserved by putting note shapes somewhere above or below a single line. This was soon found to be inadequate and the need arose for indicating more precisely the exact relativity of the sounds. More lines were added until the stave reached the unwieldy proportions of eleven lines. These were then divided – the top five for high voices or instruments (treble clef) and the other five for low voices or instruments (bass clef), leaving the middle line to register the same pitched note for either clef.

In using this single line approach with young children the same drawback applies to this method as to the last in that it must initially happen in a vacuum with very little link between this and practical musical experience. The single line can also be somewhat confusing to those who are accustomed to seeing the full stave. However, some people have found it helpful for children. With this approach it must be decided which of the five lines this single line represents and which sound, as subsequent note relationships will be affected by it.

The manner of proceeding from this beginning is to add the sounds immediately above and/or below the line and gradually to extend the lines to encompass the whole stave.

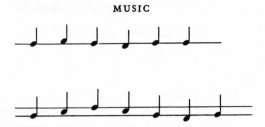

8 Recorders

It is, of course, possible to play a recorder without learning to read music but progress and repertoire are then severely handicapped. Learning the recorder has certainly been the means by which countless children have learnt notation and by offering the particular advantage notation-wise of beginning on the note B which is the middle line of the stave, it provides a stable anchor in what is sometimes the troubled sea of music reading. Further details as to the approach to notation through the use of recorder are contained in Chapter 6.

Writing music

This develops out of the reading situation and will vary according to the stage reached. In learning to read music children are being equipped with the tool for writing it. There are few problems of actual note formation – most children can draw notes from quite a young age and enjoy doing it, and as they become accustomed to seeing the notes and playing they will experiment with writing them. There would not appear to be the close correlation in music that exists between word reading and writing.

The teacher

Finally, who is to teach this music reading that will enable children to become musically literate? There are certainly not enough music specialists to do it and, if there were, they could not be in every class every day. Since it can only succeed if it is done 'little and often' it would seem that the class teacher is the ideal person. I firmly believe that many an infant and lower junior teacher would be able to do this if they were prepared to learn alongside the children and make use of some of these ideas as a teach-yourself scheme. Music in these terms has something to offer the teacher as well as the children.

General guide to lesson planning

Where music takes place at a set period of time, instead of being introduced incidentally throughout the day (which is ideal for infants), the following points are worth remembering:

Always keep a finger on the class pulse and vary the activity as needed. It is better to make a change while children are still wanting more than to continue until they have had more than enough.

As far as possible, have a cross-section of musical activity so as to include rhythm and pitch development, singing, instrumental work and some form of listening.

Try to alternate corporate and individual or group participation.

See that every child is actively participating most of the time.

Avoid singing too many verses of a song on each occasion.

Aim to think of a new approach in presenting the same idea at least once a month.

Consolidate previous learning, but also let the children attempt something new each time.

Do not expect children to sit for too long a period at a time on the floor – especially infants. If there is not room to move about, at least let them occasionally stand or be involved in some kind of bodily movement.

Fifteen to twenty minutes is long enough for most infants at any one session.

Sometimes with older children give a whole period (depending on its length) to one aspect: (a) singing – unison, rounds, parts, with tuned/untuned accompaniment; (b) a topic such as a cantata; (c) creative work – as long as it can be organized so that everyone is properly involved.

Enjoy what you do so that the children do the same.

As previously mentioned, no one would be expected to include all the aspects of music set out in this book on every occasion. Nevertheless, a balanced programme of musical activities will best give children an all-round understanding of music.

To those who feel that the timetable is already too full, I would make the plea that they seriously reconsider what music can offer at least in terms of its therapeutic value. Ten minutes a day not only gives opportunity for enjoyment but can also work wonders for teachers and children alike in releasing tension and revitalizing every situation – it has been proved, over and over again!

Recommended Books

For the teacher

A Young Teacher's Guide to Class Music, Gordon Reynolds and A. Chatterley (Novello 1969).

Musical Instruments in the Classroom, G. Winter (Education Today Series, Longman 1967).

When Word Sing, R. Murray Schafer (Universal).

The Composer in the Classroom, R. Murray Schafer (Universal).

Sound and Silence: Classroom Projects in Creative Music, John Paynter and Peter Aston (Cambridge University Press 1970).

Creative Singing, Ken Evans (Oxford University Press 1971).

Music Reading for Young Children, Florence Windbank (Novello 1966).

Dance and Dance Drama in Education, Vi Bruce (Pergamon 1965).

Movement in Silence and Sound, Vi Bruce (Bell 1970).

Words and Music (Teacher's Book), I. Lawrence and P. Montgomery (Longman 1971).

Children Make Music (Teacher's Book), Richard Addison (Holmes McDougall 1968).

The Oxford School Music Books (Teacher's Book), R. Fiske and J. P. B. Dobbs (Oxford University Press).

Growing up with music: Musical Experiences in the Infant School, Mary Pape (Oxford University Press 1970).

Discovering Music with Young Children, E. Bailey (Methuen 1958).

Text books for teacher and/or children

Begin Making Music, Richard Addison (Holmes McDougall 1968).

Make Music, Richard Addison (Holmes McDougall 1968).

Make More Music, Richard Addison (Holmes McDougall 1968).

Sounds and Music, R. E. Masters (Macmillan 1967).

Sounds and the Orchestra, R. E. Masters (Macmillan 1967).

Sound, Heat and Structures, F. F. Blackwell (*Science Project Experiments*) (Collins 1970).

How and Why – Sound (Transworld Publishers London).

101 Tunes to Explore, A. Chatterley and Gordon Reynolds (Novello).

Listening to Music: With Material for Classroom Lessons, Keith Newsom (Warne 1967).

Listening Together, N. Eele (Novello).

Introduction to Words and Music, I. Lawrence and P. Montgomery (Longman 1971).

Music Together Books 1–3, G. Winter (Longman 1968).

Music is Fun Books 1–5, D. Maxwell-Timmins (Schofield & Sims 1969–70).

Discovering Music (Books 1–4), R. G. Carter (Ginn 1966).

Music for Children – (Books 1–5 and Teacher's manual), Orff Schulwerk (Schott).

Lively Craft Cards (improvised instruments), Peter H. M. Williams (Mills & Boon 1970).

Help Yourself to Make Music, Girl Guides Association.

Song Books

Infant Music for the Nursery School, L. F. Chesterman (Harrap 1935).

This Little Puffin: Finger Plays and Nursery Games, Elizabeth Matterson (Ed.) (Penguin 1969).

Singing Fun, Lusille F. Wood and L. B. Scott (Harrap 1962).

Junior

Sing Together, W. Appleby and F. Fowler (Oxford University Press 1967).

Pentatonic Song Book, Brocklehurst (Schott).

Firsts and Seconds, W. Appleby and F. Fowler (Oxford University Press 1964).

BBC Music Broadcast pamphlets

Rounds

A First Round Book, Simpson (Novello).

Sing a Round, Mabel Wilson (Oxford University Press 1964).

Rounds and Canons (Books 1 and 2), le Fleming (Mills).

Rounds from Many Countries, Anderson (Chappell).

Graded Rounds for Recorders/Voices (Books 1 and 2), Anne Mendoza (Novello).

Round and Round Again, Harold Newman (Hargail Music Press – Universal).

Songs with instrumental ensemble accompaniment

Tops and Tails, Anne Mendoza (Oxford University Press 1968).

More Tops and Tails, Anne Mendoza (Oxford University Press 1968).

70 Simple Songs with Ostinati, Chatterly (Novello).

Sociable Songs (Book I set A and B), Anne Mendoza (Oxford University Press 1970).

Sociable Songs (Book II), Anne Mendoza (Oxford University Press 1970).

Folk Tunes to Accompany (Books 1–4, guitar), Noble (Novello).

Other Ensemble Series

Published by Chesters, Novello, Chappell, Belwin Mills, Oxford University Press.

BBC Music Broadcast Pamphlets.

Recorders (beginning stage)

Play and Sing (Books 1 and 2), Richard Addison (Holmes McDougall 1970).

Sing a Song, Play a Song, F. Dinn (Schott).

Play Tune, Margo Fagan (Longman 1973).

Pleasure and Practice with the Recorder, (Books 1–6), Leslie Winters (E. J. Arnold).

A Baker's Dozen; Nursery Rhymes; Traditional Tunes; Folk Tunes, Great Times (tuned percussion and guitar), David Clover (Feldman)